AMERICAN WAR LIBRARY

✳ **The Korean War** ✳

LIFE OF AN AMERICAN SOLDIER

by Diane Yancey

LUCENT BOOKS®

THOMSON

GALE

San Diego • Detroit • New York • San Francisco • Cleveland • New Haven, Conn. • Waterville, Maine • London • Munich

LIBRARY OF CONGRESS CATALOGING-IN-PUBLICATION DATA

Yancey, Diane.
    Life of an American soldier / by Diane Yancey.
        p. cm. — (American war library. Korean War)
Summary: Discusses the lives of American soldiers during the Korean Conflict, the kind
of war they fought, and the distress caused by returning home to find that their efforts
went virtually unnoticed.
Includes bibliographical references and index.
    ISBN 1-59018-259-6 (hardcover: alk. paper)
1. Korean War, 1950–1953—Participation, American—Juvenile literature. 2. United
States. Army—History—Korean War, 1950–1953—Juvenile literature. [1. Korean War,
1950–1953—Participation, American. 2. Soldiers. 3. United States. Army—Military life.]
I. Title. II. Series.
    DS919.Y36 2004
    951.904'2373—dc22
                                                                    2003012893

★ Contents ★

A Nation Forged by War

he United States, like many nations, was forged and defined by war. Despite Benjamin Franklin's opinion that "There never was a good war or a bad peace," the United States owes its very existence to the War of Independence, one to which Franklin wholeheartedly subscribed. The country forged by war in 1776 was tempered and made stronger by the Civil War in the 1860s.

The Texas Revolution, the Mexican-American War, and the Spanish-American War expanded the country's borders and gave it overseas possessions. These wars made the United States a world power, but this status came with a price, as the nation became a key but reluctant player in both World War I and World War II.

Each successive war further defined the country's role on the world stage. Following World War II, U.S. foreign policy redefined itself to focus on the role of defender, not only of the freedom of its own citizens, but also of the freedom of people everywhere. During the Cold War that followed World War II until the collapse of the Soviet Union, defending the world meant fighting communism. This goal, manifested in the Korean and Vietnam conflicts, proved elusive and soured the American public on its achievability. As the United States emerges as the world's sole superpower, American foreign policy has been guided less by national interest and more by protecting international human rights. But as involvement in Somalia and Kosovo proves, this goal has been equally elusive.

As a result, the country's view of itself changed. Bolstered by victories in World Wars I and II, Americans first relished the role of protector. But, as war followed war in a seemingly endless procession, Americans began to doubt their leaders, their motives, and themselves. The Vietnam War especially caused people to question the validity of sending its young people to die in places where they were not particularly wanted and for people who did not seem especially grateful.

While the most obvious changes brought about by America's wars have been geopolitical in nature, many other aspects of society have been touched. War often does not bring about change directly, but acts instead like the catalyst in a chemical reaction, accelerating changes already in progress.

Some of these changes have been societal. The role of women in the United States had been slowly changing, but World War II put thousands into the work force and into uniform. They might have gone back to being housewives after the war, but equality, once experienced, would not be forgotten.

Likewise, wars have accelerated technological change. The necessity for faster airplanes and more destructive bombs led to the development of jet planes and nuclear energy. Artificial fibers developed for parachutes in the 1940s were used in clothing of the 1950s.

Lucent Books' American War Library covers key wars in the development of the nation. Each war is covered in several volumes, to allow for more detail, context, and to provide volumes on often neglected subjects, such as the kamikazes of World War II, or the weapons used in the Civil War. As with all Lucent books, notes, annotated bibliographies, and appendixes such as glossaries give students a launching point for further research. In addition, sidebars and archival photographs enhance the text. Together, each volume in The American War Library will aid students in understanding how America's wars have shaped and changed its politics, economics, and society.

The War That Never Was

Since 1953, stone-faced North Korean soldiers have been standing guard over a 156-mile-long stretch of land known as the Demilitarized Zone (DMZ)—the meeting place between the Democratic People's Republic of Korea (North Korea) and the Republic of Korea (South Korea). The zone lies roughly east-west along the 38th parallel, is 2.5 miles wide, and is edged by 8-foot-high barbed wire fences. Just south of it are U.S. troops who, like earlier soldiers, help police one of the most tension-filled locales in the world.

The DMZ was formed to keep opposing armies apart at the end of the Korean War. It stands as a symbol of the deep political and philosophical differences that divided the Communist North Korea and the democratic United States throughout the second half of the twentieth century. It also represents uneasy compromises made in a war that was never formally declared and never completely resolved. Be-

cause of it, thousands of U.S. troops have been rotated in and out of Korea over the years. As author Joseph C. Goulden writes, "From time to time the new generation of soldiers asks, 'What am I doing in this obscure little part of the world?'"[1] It is a question that many Americans have posed since the Korean War began more than fifty years ago.

The Domino Theory

Sometimes known as "the war that never was," the Korean conflict was technically a police action, called into play by President Harry Truman after North Korea invaded South Korea in June 1950. Like many Americans, Truman believed in the "domino theory"—the presumption that if one country's government fell to communism, the governments of neighboring nations would soon topple like a row of dominoes. The Soviet Union had experienced a Communist revolution in 1917. The Soviets had established the

Communist North Korean government in 1948. Korea's neighbor China had had its own Communist revolution in 1949. If nothing were done, South Korea appeared to be the domino most likely to fall next. Truman stated in 1951,

> The threat of world conquest by Soviet Russia endangers our liberty and endangers the kind of world in which the free spirit of man can survive. This threat is aimed at all peoples who strive to win or defend their own freedom and national independence. Indeed, the state of our Nation is in great part the state of our friends and allies throughout the world. The gun that points at them points at us, also. The threat is a total threat and the danger is a common danger. All free nations are exposed and all are in peril.[2]

Faced with a crisis, Truman authorized military action. U.S. troops were

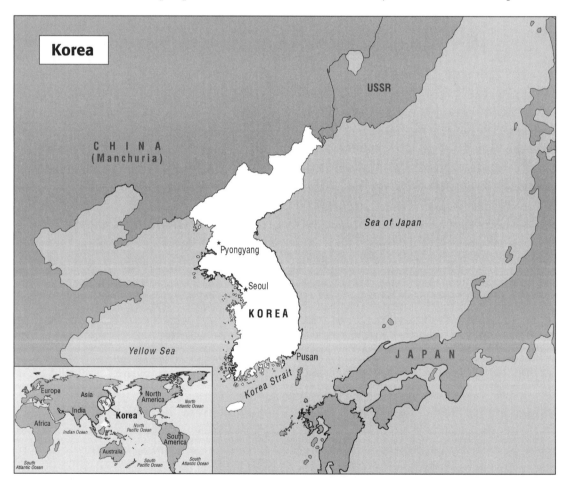

sent into Korea to combat the invaders. The first five hundred army troops to arrive, however, had no notion of the task they were undertaking—holding back a ferocious invading force until reinforcements could arrive. They were ill-informed and totally unprepared for the demands made on them. Philip Day Jr., who came to Korea as a lieutenant with the Twenty-first Infantry on July 1, 1950, recalls, "No one believed we were going anywhere to fight. I sort of had the impression we were going to protect and help Americans leaving the country."[3]

"A Sour Little War"

Despite being unprepared for war, U.S. troops and most Americans supported U.S. involvement in Korea at first. They believed that communism posed a threat to the world and that freedom and democracy were worth defending. "I felt like a shining knight in bright armor," says Phil Woods. "They were communists, we were a free society. We were there to protect a small independent nation that was getting picked on by bullies."[4]

That idealism faded as soldiers met fierce resistance from North Koreans and hundreds of thousands of Communist Chinese who joined the war. U.S. troops quickly learned that fighting in Korea was one of the most difficult and unrewarding tasks they would ever undertake. They faced a determined enemy, restrictions that made winning the war impossible, and a harsh environment. The terrain

A New Kind of War

Although Korea is remembered as an "unimportant" war, it was unique in one important way, as author Donald Knox points out in *The Korean War: Uncertain Victory*.

> The Korean War was the first America ever waged that was not fought for national survival, for territory, for Manifest Destiny, or for hegemony [domination]. Korea was the first *ideological* war. For the first time in the nation's history, Americans were asked to fight and die to contain an *idea*. . . .
>
> As the first postnuclear war, Korea was fought under strictures [restrictions] designed to keep the conflict limited. The men in Washington were never certain that the war with China would not erupt with sudden fury into a nuclear confrontation with the Soviets. With hindsight one may question their choices, but the fact that such choices had to be made tells us something about the nature of war in the last half of the twentieth century, and it affected forever the manner in which military decisions must now be made.

was mountainous. Monsoon rains turned the ground to mud. Temperatures soared in the summer and dropped well below freezing in the winter. Diplomat W. Averill Harriman eventually decided that the fight was "a sour little war,"[5] while Secretary of State Dean Acheson observed, "If the best minds in the world had set out to find us the worst possible location in the world to fight . . . the unanimous choice would have been Korea."[6]

Fighting men could only hope that they would come through the conflict alive so that they could return home. Those who did were hurt to find that their homecoming went virtually unnoticed. The war had had no effect on ordinary citizens who had enjoyed the benefits of peace and prosperity in the United States. As one soldier wrote in 1952: "The U.S. was aware of the conflict in Korea only in the sense that taxes were higher. The soldiers in Korea envied those at home living in a nation mentally at peace while physically at war."[7]

The experiences and sacrifices of the men and women who fought in the Korean War have remained unappreciated. Yet their endeavors made them some of the most admirable fighting forces anywhere. Author Victor Hicken notes in *The American Fighting Man*:

In some ways the performance of the American fighting man in Korea was nothing short of miraculous. Most of the men fought solely out of a sense of duty, and possibly pride. They fought while politicians back home told them that the war was useless, they sacrificed while friends back home enjoyed a general prosperity brought on by the war, they fought under military and political restraint, and they gave battle under some of the most miserable climatic conditions ever faced by American warriors.[8]

The account of these men's struggles, their achievements, their patriotism, and their service is the story of American soldiers in the Korean War.

Chapter 1

Prologue to Action

American soldiers did not expect to have to fight another war just five years after World War II drew to a close. Those veterans who had served in Europe and the Pacific were tired of battle and wanted to concentrate on their families, their jobs, and their futures. Those enlistees who joined the service after 1945 had done so in the belief that the enemy was defeated and peace would be the norm for many years. "The recruiting posters that had induced most of these men to enter the Army mentioned all conceivable advantages and promised many good things, but never suggested that the principal business of an army is to fight,"[9] observes military historian Lieutenant Colonel Roy E. Appleman.

Although all Americans shared the desire for peace, most people were fearful that Communist aggression would soon threaten their own shores. The Soviet Union had newly-developed atomic weapons, and many feared they would be used against the West with deadly effect. Many also believed that a show of military might was the only thing that would prevent such devastation. Thus, when unexpected problems arose in Korea in 1950, a strong display of force seemed necessary to defuse the threat quickly and completely. Few realized that that display would be the prologue to a long war and that American soldiers would be stationed in the country for decades to come.

Early Tensions

The American military first became involved in Korean affairs while dismantling the Japanese empire at the end of World War II. Japan had ruled Korea since 1910 and controlled its 21 million inhabitants with a large army that ruthlessly squashed resistance and efforts to gain independence. When Japan was defeated at the end of the war, both the Soviet Union and American troops entered Korea, ostensibly to help establish order

Divided Korea

war drew to a close, hostility grew between the two countries due to the actions of Soviet dictator Joseph Stalin. The Communist leader sent his armies to invade and occupy countries in Eastern Europe and sponsored Communist attempts to conquer Greece, Iran, and Turkey. In 1947, Stalin blocked all movement between northern and southern parts of Korea at the 38th parallel. The actions caused President Truman to call for a stop to the spread of communism. The ensuing ideological struggle between the United States and the Soviets, coupled with an arms race including nuclear weapons, spying, propaganda, and political deception, became known as the Cold War.

Early in the Cold War, the Soviet Union began building the North Korean army into a large, well-equipped fighting force. The United States did not do the same in South Korea, but did station fifty thousand American troops there between 1945 and 1948. This occupation force helped round up

and a new government. The Soviets entered from the north, while American troops landed in the south.

The Soviets had been allies of the United States in World War II, but as the and deport Japanese troops, stabilize the country while a new government was being formed, and prevent infiltration of Communists from the north. Clinton E. Berryhill, an eighteen-year-old with the Thirty-second Infantry Regiment in 1947, recalls his experiences there: "I was a scout, sniper and squad leader in the Intelligence and Reconnaissance Platoon of the Thirty-second's HQ [Headquarters] Company based in Seoul. The regiment was grossly under strength, and living conditions were primitive. Russians broadcast that they would wipe us out. We were ready to fight, but thankfully war never came then."[10]

In 1948, Korean leader Kim Il Sung was established as head of the Democratic People's Republic of Korea, the Soviet-sponsored government of North Korea. Soviet forces pulled out of North Korea and, at the same time, challenged the U.S. military to do the same in the south. In response, in May 1948 the United Nations organized parliamentary elections in South Korea. Syngman Rhee was elected president of the new Republic of Korea (ROK), and U.S. troops were withdrawn by June 1949, leaving only a few military advisers behind.

Conditions were not peaceful on the Korean peninsula, however. Neither Sung's nor Rhee's government recognized the legitimacy of the other, and the two countries skirmished periodically. Because

Leader of North Korea Kim Il Sung (left) and President of South Korea Syngman Rhee (right) did not share the same political vision for a unified nation.

Rhee repeatedly threatened to take his 115,000-man army, march on the north, and unify all of Korea, the United States continued to limit the military aid it provided him to light artillery and ammunition. The Soviet Union, on the other hand, continued to fortify the North Korean army. By the spring of 1950, it was a force of 150,000 ground soldiers equipped with tanks and heavy artillery.

Invasion!

The United States half-feared that Rhee would start a war in Korea, but it was the North Korean People's Army (NKPA) that launched a heavy artillery barrage across the 38th parallel in the early morning hours of June 25, 1950. Rhee had fortified the line with his best troops, but even they could not stop the invasion that followed. By 9:30 A.M. amphibious landings (landings by sea) were being made on the east coast south of Kangnung, and the town of Kaesong had fallen.

Captain Joseph R. Darrigo, one of the few U.S. military advisers left in the country, was awakened when fragments of a North Korean artillery shell struck his house along the border near Kaesong. He hurried into town and was stunned to see a regiment of North Korean soldiers stepping off a train that had just pulled into the station. They opened fire on him, but Darrigo was able to get away and report the situation.

The ominous news soon spread. Despite its menacing sound, however, few U.S. servicemen took it seriously. Corporal Lacy Barnett remembers, "When word reached us in Japan on that rainy Sunday, the first reaction by many members of my unit was, 'Where is Korea?' The next reaction, 'Let the gooks [derogatory slang for Asians] kill each other off.' Among the majority of men there was absolutely no fear or thought that the United States would become involved in the war."[11]

President Truman was relaxing at his home in Independence, Missouri, when he received a call notifying him that an invasion was taking place. He recognized the seriousness of the event. "In my generation, this was not the first occasion when the strong had attacked the weak," he observes in his memoirs:

> I felt certain that if south Korea was allowed to fall Communist leaders would be emboldened to override nations closer to our own shores. . . . If this were allowed to go unchallenged it would mean a third world war, just as similar incidents had brought on the second world war.[12]

Because the United Nations had been involved in the formation of South Korea, Truman notified the UN Security Council. The president knew, however, that he would have to take action as well. Thus, on June 27, after the Security Council voted unanimously to call for the immediate withdrawal of North Korean forces from South Korea, Truman told Congress that he had authorized the use of U.S. air and naval units to attack any North Koreans who were south of the 38th parallel.

Because only Congress had authority to declare war, Truman called the military deployment a "UN police action." "We are not at war," he stated at a press conference on June 29, 1950: "The Republic of Korea was set up with the United Nations help. . . . It was unlawfully attacked by a bunch of bandits which are neighbors of North Korea. . . . The members of the United Nations are going to the relief of the Korean Republic to suppress a bandit raid on the Republic of Korea."[13]

War Generals

On July 10 the UN Security Council voted to establish a UN Command to coordinate military efforts to defend South Korea. General Douglas MacArthur, commander of the U.S. Far East Command based in Japan, was put in charge of the war. MacArthur was a charismatic but egotistical war hero who had been Supreme Allied Commander in the Pacific in World War II. His belief in himself made him a strong and successful leader, although it sometimes caused him to take positions and risks that another man would have avoided. "There is no security on this earth, there is only opportunity,"[14] he once said.

The chances that the general took with his men during the Inchon invasion in Korea in September 1950 illustrated his audaciousness. The location of the invasion, launched behind enemy lines, was especially tricky due to the low tides in the harbor. The moment of attack had to be precisely timed or ships would be stuck in the mud and only part of the invading force would be able to land. High tide, however, was just before sunset, leaving men little time to land, link up, and establish their defenses before dark. "Everyone was very apprehensive about this landing," remembers Captain Francis Fenton Jr. "It really looked dangerous. There was a finger pier and a causeway extending out from RED Beach . . . and if machine guns were on the finger pier and causeway, we were going to have a tough time making the last 200 yards to the beach."[15]

Despite many extremely dangerous moments, the invasion was successfully carried out, enhancing MacArthur's reputation as a superb military leader. Over time, however, his outspoken conviction

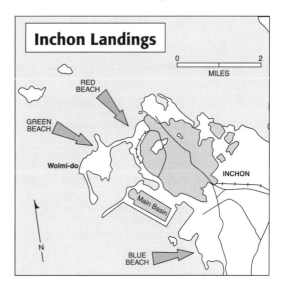

Inchon Landings

0   2
MILES

RED BEACH

GREEN BEACH

Wolmi-do

INCHON

Main Basin

N

BLUE BEACH

Four U.S. landing ship tanks (LSTs) unload men and military equipment onto Red Beach during the Inchon invasion.

that Korea should be reunited no matter what the cost as well as his habit of ignoring orders from his superiors caused serious problems between the general and Truman.

Truman and MacArthur first disagreed in July 1950 over the way the war should be fought. MacArthur not only wanted to defeat the North Korean invaders and unify Korea, he also repeatedly implied that the United States would welcome the involvement of Chiang Kai-shek's Chinese Nationalist government (opponent of the Communist Chinese, headquartered in Taiwan) in the Korean conflict. He even

hinted that an invasion of mainland Communist China could be possible.

The statements angered Truman, who was more moderate in his views. He believed that an invasion of China might invite World War III and nuclear holocaust. He was willing to forgo the use of America's nuclear weapons, limit the war to Korea, and even accept a divided Korea if that would restore peace. He was also outraged that MacArthur was refusing to honor him as head military policy maker in the nation. He chose to overlook MacArthur's statements for a time, however, because the Inchon invasion was so successful and because the general was so popular with the military and the American public.

Eventually, MacArthur pushed Truman too far by calling on General Peng Teh-huai, the Communist Chinese commander in North Korea, to surrender or be prepared for an invasion of China.

Faced with a loose cannon, the president relieved MacArthur of his duties on April 11, 1951, saying "General MacArthur is one of our greatest military commanders, but the cause of world peace is much more important than any individual."[16]

Truman chose Lieutenant General Matthew Ridgway, an experienced World War II commander who had led airborne units in Sicily and Normandy, to replace MacArthur and lead the UN Command. Ridgway had been in charge of the Eighth

MacArthur's Farewell

On April 19, 1951, on the eve of his retirement, General Douglas MacArthur delivered a famous farewell speech to the U.S. Congress, excerpted here. He used that speech, which can be read in its entirety on the American Rhetoric website, to make the case that he had been unfairly removed from leadership.

> While I was not consulted prior to the President's decision to intervene in support of the Republic of Korea, that decision from a military standpoint, proved a sound one, as we hurled back the invader and decimated [reduced] his forces. Our victory was complete, and our objectives within reach, when Red China intervened with numerically superior ground forces.
>
> This created a new war and an entirely new situation, . . . a situation which called for new decisions in the diplomatic sphere to permit the realistic adjustment of military strategy.
>
> Such decisions have not been forthcoming.
>
> I called for reinforcements but was informed that reinforcements were not available. I made clear that if not permitted to destroy the enemy built-up bases north of the Yalu [River], if not permitted to utilize the friendly Chinese Force of some 600,000 men on Formosa, if not permitted to blockade the China coast to prevent the Chinese Reds from getting succor from without, and if there were to be no hope of major reinforcements, the position of the command from the military standpoint forbade victory. . . .
>
> Efforts have been made to distort my position. It has been said, in effect, that I was a warmonger. Nothing could be further from the truth. I know war as few other men now living know it, and nothing to me is more revolting. I have long advocated its complete abolition. . . .
>
> But once war is forced upon us, there is no other alternative than to apply every available means to bring it to a swift end.
>
> War's very object is victory, not prolonged indecision.
>
> In war there is no substitute for victory.

Army—all American forces on the ground in South Korea—since December 26, 1950, and his strong leadership and ability to bring out the best in men had boosted army confidence and renewed his troops' fighting spirit just when heavy defeats left them discouraged. "Ridgway

Lieutenant General Matthew B. Ridgway (right) inspects the Korean battlefront after replacing General Douglas MacArthur as head of the UN Command.

took hold of the Eighth Army, grabbed it by the throat, gave it a good shake, and straightened it out," says retired marine commander Edwin Simmons:

> If you had looked at a situation map at the end of December, 1950, you would have seen little blue dots all over the peninsula, little isolated U.N. positions—no sign of coherence or integrity. He shook all that out. He reformed a line across the peninsula

from one coast to the other, and then he began a deliberate, buttoned-up offensive a step at a time.[17]

Ridgway's opportunity to earn fame as a fighter comparable to MacArthur faded in 1951, however, after peace talks began. The war settled into a stalemate at the 38th parallel, and the general concluded that dramatic offensives would only result in high casualty rates without a chance of decisive victory. Lieutenant Marvin Muskat observed in the winter of 1951–1952, "This was a war that was going nowhere. No advances. General Ridgway had specifically ordered that there should be no offensive action, so the line was supposed to be static. . . . [Action] wasn't intended to take ground, only to kill the enemy."[18]

On May 12, 1952, Ridgway was promoted to the post of Supreme Commander of the Allied Powers in Europe, and was replaced by General Mark Clark, a veteran of both world wars. Clark headed the UN Command in Korea until 1953, and took part in the signing of an armistice between the warring parties on July 27 of that year.

Help Is on the Way

As head of military forces, on June 29, 1950, MacArthur flew to the South Korean capital of Seoul to assess the situation. He found the city in flames and the ROK army in retreat. Rightly believing that the situation was extremely serious, he was nevertheless convinced that the introduction of U.S. ground troops could reverse the invasion. "If those asses back in Washington only will not hobble me, I can handle it with one arm tied behind my back,"[19] he boasted.

Truman gave MacArthur the go-ahead to send troops into Korea, and the general passed the word to his commanders. Nevertheless, finding men ready to fight a war immediately was somewhat difficult. U.S. military strength had shrunk in numbers from over 12 million to about 1.5 million since the end of World War II in 1945. Much of that military force was stationed in Europe, where growing pressure from the Soviet Union on East European countries made a strong military presence necessary.

Some U.S. soldiers were stationed in occupied Japan, but these were no longer combat-ready forces: In five years, discipline and training had slackened. They enjoyed a very comfortable lifestyle because the economy of Japan was weak, and anyone with U.S. dollars could afford many luxuries. Private First Class Robert Roy, for example, was "living the good life" on the island of Kyushu with few responsibilities when the Korean War broke out:

As a PFC I was only getting about eighty dollars a month, but that was plenty. That was more than enough to live good. You could live off the base in a Japanese house for ten dollars a month, with a girl to do all the cooking and cleaning and laundry. . . . You could go on liberty every night. . . . There were bars and movie theaters and cabarets where you could drink beer and talk with the girls.[20]

Army logistics finally mustered five hundred men who could leave for Korea immediately. They included two rifle companies, a headquarters company, and a heavy weapons company of the army's 24th Infantry Division. They were dubbed Task Force Smith after their commander, Lieutenant Colonel Charles Smith. Although this was nowhere near the number of men that MacArthur needed, and some Task Force Smith troops had spent their time in service as clerks and cooks, MacArthur was convinced that just the sight of Americans would be "an arrogant display of strength"[21] that would badly frighten the enemy. He also believed Task Force Smith would help improve the ROK army's morale and stiffen its resistance until more U.S. forces arrived.

New Recruits

As Task Force Smith made its way to Korea, American soldiers stationed in the United States were told that they too would soon be heading overseas. Even men who had served in World War II were called up again. Those who were new recruits had to go through basic training before they were equipped to fight, however.

Basic training in the late 1940s was not always the rigorous instruction that it had been in World War II and would be again in the Vietnam era. Young men who had enlisted for education benefits or a chance to get away from home and see the world did not always take the daily drilling, instruction, and field training seriously. Anthony B. Herbert, who trained in Fort Dix, New Jersey, recalls his days there: "I had a pretty good time in basic. We were paid for fun and games—fresh air and exercise, a couple of boring classes, some dismounted drill, a little first-aid, rifle and heavy weapons training, a bivouac [camp out], some marches, and a lot of laughs."[22]

As the Cold War escalated, the draft was reactivated. From 1948 until 1951, 19-to-26-year-olds could be inducted for twenty-one months' service in the army, to be followed by five years of reserve duty. In 1951, length of service was extended to twenty-four months, and the minimum age for induction was reduced to 18.5 years.

With the nation at war, recruits began to take basic training more seriously. Along with discipline and drill, they spent weeks concentrating on tactics, operating and maintaining heavy equipment, throwing hand grenades, and the like. Private Arnold Winter, a member of the 1st Provisional Marine Brigade, was one of many who worked hard:

There was the fear of disobeying an order. . . . When they gave you an order to go, you went, in spite of everything. And there was also the

Unexpected Assignment

Men like Sergeant C.W. "Bill" Menninger were caught off guard when Truman called up troops to serve again in South Korea. In Donald Knox's *The Korean War: Pusan to Chosin*, Menninger describes exactly what he was doing when his call came.

> When the invasion of the south came, of course everyone was interested, but it never occurred to us that we Americans serving in Japan in the Army of Occupation would ever get involved. For me, it was a typical Sunday night in Japan. I was at home with my family. It had rained all day. My wife was giving the kids a bath prior to putting them to bed, and I was reading a book and nursing a drink when the call came for me to report at once to headquarters! The wife wanted to know what the call was about. "Something must be wrong with next week's training schedule," I answered. "I'll be back as soon as I can." (Which happened to be eleven months later.)

fear of letting your buddies down. There's an almost unbelievable loyalty among men in a rifle company, and you don't want to be the guy to break that bond. You didn't want to die, but you also didn't want to embarrass yourself by failing your buddies.[23]

As there would be in the Vietnam War, there was some draft evasion during the Korean War, especially as support for the conflict waned in 1952 and 1953. About eighty thousand draft evasion cases were investigated. Political activism was not as strong in 1950 as it was during the Vietnam era, however, and those who resisted often did so because of religious or philosophical convictions. Such was the case of James Lawson, a civil rights advocate who was also a pacifist. Willing to face the consequences of his resistance, he explains, "I sent my draft cards back to the local board and said that I would not cooperate with the classification process. That meant that in 1950 the FBI arrested me, and in 1951 I was tried in the federal court in Cleveland, Ohio, and sentenced to three years in prison."[24]

Back to Service

While new recruits trained and waited nervously for a chance to test their courage in the war, those men who had served in World War II knew what they were heading for when they were called back to service in Korea. They had fought in Europe and the South Pacific, and realized how hard it was to defeat a determined, well-equipped enemy. Some had battled their way through strongly defended German positions in both World Wars I and II. Others had fought their way ashore on dozens of jungle islands that were held by Japanese forces in the Pacific.

Veterans knew the hardships and the horrors of war, but they also knew how a war could be successfully fought. Major Ed Simmons remembers,

> [In Camp Pendleton, California,] we got the replacements we needed to build the division up to war strength. . . .

Morale Builder

After being placed in charge of a discouraged Eighth Army in December 1950, General Matthew Ridgway set out to rebuild morale in a variety of practical ways. His words are included in Rod Paschall's book *Witness to War: Korea*.

> Within forty-eight hours or so, I had visited every corps and division commander. . . . [The UN commanders] knew if I was up there, if I was up there myself, my principal purpose was to get the quickest and most accurate picture of the situation and to help them, not interfere in any way, but to help them. Particularly, I found this in the early stages, they weren't using more than a third of the firepower they had available to them. It was back in the column on the road somewhere, but unused. . . .

> I asked one man what his particular gripe was. He wanted to write home but he never got any stationery to write on. So, I had somebody send up a supply of stationery to that particular unit that night marked for this soldier. . . . I would take extra pairs of gloves along. . . . Any soldier up there—you know—the temperature is down below or around zero and his hands are cold and raw . . . the general gives his gloves to front line soldiers. . . . Word gets around about those things.

Most were World War Two veterans. They were experienced combat marines, and that's a fact that can't be made too much of. That single fact, the quality of the men who were called back to active duty . . . had a lot to do with the outstanding performance of the marines over there.[25]

Despite their experience, the war in Korea would prove an eye-opening event even for veterans. Chairman of the Joint Chiefs of Staff Omar Bradley, a World War II commander in Europe, described it as "the wrong war, in the wrong place, at the wrong time, with the wrong enemy."[26] He referred not only to the grueling fighting conditions but to the enemy's determina-tion, the limitations placed upon the fighting, and the difficulty of winning.

Sergeant Ed Hendricks, who had served in the Pacific, was more specific in naming the hardships: "We'd take the hill one day, give it back the next. The heat was the worst you ever felt. It would some-times rain. Walking in the mud was almost impossible. Many times we were sur-rounded. Got low on ammunition, noth-ing to eat. . . . Fighting was so bad medics couldn't get in to carry the dead out."[27]

It soon became clear that Korea would not be the short, easy war that MacArthur hoped for. The coming three years would test each man's courage and skill as much as involvement in any ear-lier war had done.

Chapter 2

A Shaky Beginning

MacArthur proved to be overconfident. He assumed that American forces were superior to the North Koreans both as fighters and as human beings. U.S. soldiers themselves assumed that they would win because they were fighting for a just cause. All assumptions were blown away on the first day of battle. The following months were equally demoralizing. Colonel John Michaelis, commander of the Twenty-seventh Regiment, summarized the situation:

[The men] didn't know their weapons. . . . They'd spent a lot of time listening to lectures on the difference between Communism and Americanism and not enough time crawling on their bellies on maneuvers with live ammunition singing over them. They'd been nursed and coddled, told to drive safely, to buy War Bonds, to avoid VD [venereal disease; sexually transmitted disease], to write a letter home to mother, when somebody ought to have been telling them how to clear a machine gun when it jams. They've had to learn in combat, in a matter of days, the basic things they should have known before they ever faced an enemy. And some of them don't learn fast enough.[28]

Task Force Smith

Members of Task Force Smith were the first to learn that MacArthur had overestimated their abilities and underestimated the North Koreans. The Americans arrived in Korea on July 1, 1950, and fought for the first time on July 5. Almost immediately they were overrun by a line of Korean tanks and infantry that stretched for miles. "We had a pretty good idea right then that we had something that was going to cause us a hell of a lot of woe,"[29] Smith later observed.

The task force bravely fired on the enemy, but their outdated bazookas

(portable weapons launchers), leftovers from World War II, did not make a dent in modern, Soviet-made tanks. To make matters worse, some of their machine guns, also leftovers from the war, would not fire. Radios would not function. Many of the shells they launched were old and failed to explode.

As the enemy began to surround his men, Smith ordered a hasty withdrawal. Panicking, his inexperienced force threw down their weapons and fled, leaving their wounded behind. "Normally what you do when you have to withdraw is you set up a rendezvous point," explains Robert Roy. "Then you retreat in an orderly fashion toward that point. But there was never any rendezvous point. Nobody told us anything. So we all took off on our own."[30]

Portable weapons launchers had proved to be effective during previous wars, but they were nearly useless against Soviet-built tanks in Korea.

Roy was with a squad of men who were soon captured, but he managed to remain free and rejoined the remains of Smith's command. Later, it was determined that over 150 men of Task Force Smith were killed, wounded, or missing in the first days of fighting. It was a discouraging start to the war.

First Impressions

Task Force Smith and many other regiments that later arrived in Korea were not only ignorant of the enemy and its ways but also unprepared for the country's climate, geography, and a host of other factors. Their introduction came when they arrived, by air or sea, at the port town of Pusan on the southeast coast.

As South Korea's second largest city, Pusan had a landing strip and a natural harbor where cargo ships could anchor and where flat-bottomed landing ships (LSTs) carrying men, vehicles, and even tanks could pull close to shore, open their doors, and unload. Soldiers stepped out into a country that was tiny, rural, and vastly different from the affluent, industrial United States.

Their first impressions depended strongly on the seasons. On a clear day in summer, the blue of the Sea of Japan and the green of the hills surrounding the town created a picturesque setting. Rice paddies added more lush green color. High heat and humidity made for uncomfortable weather, however, and the Korean custom of fertilizing the paddies with human excrement produced a distinctly offensive odor that filled the air. "As the ship pulled into the harbor you could smell Korea. It is said that Korea is the only country that you can smell 20 miles from its borders,"[31] observed Jake Huffaker, of the 304th Signal Battalion.

Summer flowers and shrubs colored the landscape, but summer was also a time of monsoons, when torrential rain turned dust to mud. The moisture supported enormous numbers of insects. Wasps, ticks, lice, fleas, and bedbugs were common pests. Swarms of mosquitoes and flies made newcomers constantly miserable.

One soldier noted, "The flies would carry you away. . . . We were spitting them out of our mouths as we talked."[32]

Those men who arrived in winter saw Korea as a land of brown hills, strong winds, and snow. Freezing temperatures could persist both day and night. James Brady recorded his first impressions as his plane came in for a landing in late November 1951: "Even on the low hills there was snow. Only in the flat of the valley where the plane would come down was there bare earth, brown and frozen hard. . . . Up and down the valley you could see huts and tents and a few unsuccessful fires giving no apparent heat and little light in the gray morning."[33]

"I Was Surprised"

Many troops saw Korea for the first time as participants in the invasion of Inchon, beginning on September 15, 1950. To carry out the invasion, MacArthur reactivated a unit known as X (Tenth) Corps, commanded by General Edward M. Almond. X Corps, comprising army and marine units, functioned independently of the Eighth Army (led by General Walton Walker) until after its withdrawal from North Korea in late December 1950. Then it came under the direction of the Eighth Army command.

For the men of X Corps, their first image of Korea was of misty hills coupled with heavy smoke from gunfire and the burning city of Inchon. Their landing craft entered the harbor, proceeded through a winding channel, and then allowed them to disembark on two beaches. To marine private Fred Davidson, who was one of the first to land, the sight of so many Americans coming ashore was more interesting than the new terrain: "This was fantastic! It was just like watching a John Wayne movie projected on an enormous 3-D Cinemascope screen. Not everyone can say they actually witnessed a Marine division making a landing on a beach. It was simply beautiful!"[34]

From Inchon, the capital city of Seoul was only twenty-five miles away, and with the weather clearing, troops advanced along a paved highway paralleled by a railway. Dust was soon a problem as tanks rumbled past. When they reached the outskirts of Seoul, home to over 1 million people, the troops saw the sooty chimneys of the city surrounded by rice paddies and green-brown hills. Private John Bishop's first reaction was surprise: "It looked at the time as big as New York. Up until then, walking for days and days, all we'd seen was dirt, rocks, hills, farms, and old shacks. I was surprised they even had a city."[35]

When the men finally entered Seoul, they realized that it was similar to American cities in many ways. There were gra-

Soldiers brave the winter chill while scouting the snow-covered hills and valleys of South Korea.

Close Call

American soldiers had to be on guard for guerrilla activity by North Koreans, who were capable of attacking when least expected. In Donald Knox's *The Korean War: Pusan to Chosin*, Private Doug Koch describes one close call he witnessed on the march to Seoul in September 1950.

We were sitting on a hill eating C rations when down the road comes a couple of jeeps. When they got past the tanks and were below us, they stopped. All these officers —we could see their eagles and stars— jumped out and began talking to the guys along the road. . . . This one guy was real tall. He walked closer to us. It was General

MacArthur. Boy, we were, you know, well, it was the thrill of a lifetime. . . . Pretty soon they jumped back into their jeeps and went down the road.

Soon a kid from the village near us came over and started jabbering to our interpreter. . . . The two of them climbed down to the road right where General MacArthur had stood and the interpreter hollered into a culvert. A moment later seven armed North Koreans came out of the culvert, all with their hands on their heads. Just think how famous one of them would have been if he'd lobbed a hand grenade onto the road a few minutes before and hit our generals.

cious neighborhoods and shabby ones. Modern buildings contrasted sharply with five-hundred-year-old palaces and churches. At the same time, parts of the town showed evidence of having been invaded by the North Koreans. "The city was dirty," observes Private Win Scott. "There were animals running wild and junk everywhere. . . . Pictures of Stalin hung on some of the buildings. Communist propaganda was all over."[36]

The smell of raw sewage was also unmistakable. Seoul was one of the largest cities in the world without an underground sewage system. The odor sometimes wafted all the way out to ships entering Inchon Harbor. Richard Athey, who served in a graves registration unit in Seoul, told his son Brandt Athey, "It smelled bad all the time. In particular,

this smell came from the [Han] river, where people went to the bathroom, bathed, and drank. You would see people carrying buckets and buckets of their own waste to dump in the sea."[37]

Heading for Battle

With the exception of those men who first arrived to take part in the Inchon invasion, troops entering Korea were taken to a commanding officer where they received specific assignments. Some were ordered to join fighting units that needed reinforcements. Some were given less dangerous assignments as office workers, laundry personnel, postal clerks, and other support staff on bases throughout the country.

Those headed for battle were issued guns and ammunition and then boarded on trains or trucks to the front. Railroads ran between Pusan and Seoul, and highways connected larger cities and towns. Many were congested with Korean civilians fleeing before the oncoming North Koreans, however. Marine private Herbert Luster recalls his trip to the front lines:

> The road was crowded with people who were loaded down with children and personal belongings. Fear and uncertainly were on their faces. Where were they coming from? Where were they going? They all looked so very tired—they must have walked a long way. Most of the people were going the opposite way the Marines were going. The road wasn't wide enough for two-way traffic, so the whole scene was a dusty mess.[38]

Nevertheless, U.S. soldiers were able to make their way to the fighting. "It took us four days to get into position," remembers Robert Roy. "First we were put on a train and went as far as [the town of] Taejon. At Taejon we loaded onto trucks, and from there we moved a little farther north each day."[39]

A Wily Enemy

Like the men they joined, reinforcements for Task Force Smith soon discovered that they were not prepared to fight the determined North Koreans. For months, their numbers and weaponry were inferior against tanks and heavy artillery. Some of the men had never before fired the M-1 rifles they had been issued and discovered too late that many were defective.

At the same time, all had to learn the enemy's fighting style. At times the North Koreans attacked head-on with tanks while portions of their infantry flanked the Americans and came in from behind, encircling them and cutting off their retreat. At other times, the enemy would adopt guerrilla tactics such as dressing in civilian clothing and then ambushing U.S. troops. Unable to tell civilians from enemy soldiers, American troops became jittery and prone to shoot anyone who looked suspicious. Many innocent civilians were injured or killed as a result.

Other North Korean guerrilla tactics, such as striking out of the darkness or popping out of one-man foxholes to shoot or toss grenades, took the Americans by surprise as well. "The underbrush was so thick that [a buddy] and I got only about ten feet from a gook's hole when an arm came out of it and lobbed a grenade in our direction. It landed right next to me. It was a dud,"[40] recalls Private James Cardinal.

When Communist Chinese forces (CCF) later entered the war, they proved to be well trained in guerrilla warfare as well. Masters of concealment, they hid during the day and fought at night, appearing out of the darkness in human wave assaults, during which group after group of fighters charged forward, sacrificing themselves until Americans ran out of ammunition and were overwhelmed.

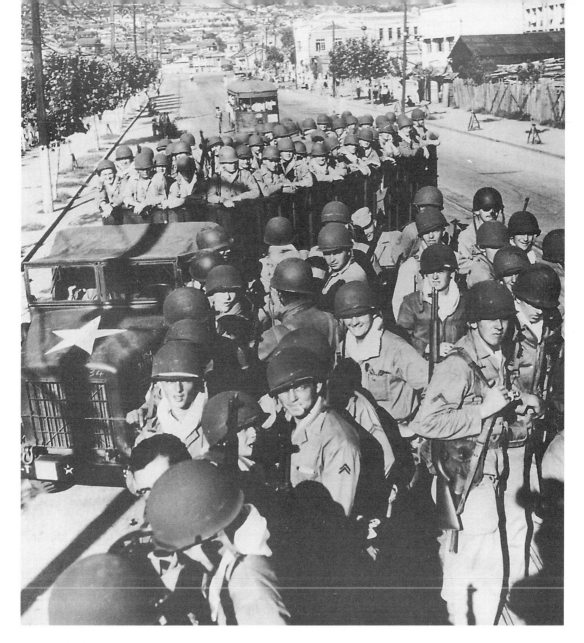

Newly arrived U.S. Marines near Pusan board trucks that will take them to the battlefront.

Instead of using radio communications, most used an unnerving mix of bugles, whistles, and colored rockets to communicate with and signal each other, and the unexpected sights and sounds coupled with the massed night assaults psychologically undermined the resistance of U.S. forces.

"Bugout Fever"

Once MacArthur saw that victory would not be quick or easy, he was resigned to ordering the first U.S. troops to carry out

a delaying action until additional forces arrived. Hard fighting occurred on July 19 and 20 in the battle for Taejon, a crucial crossroads 100 miles south of Seoul. The North Koreans assaulted the Americans with fighter planes, tanks, and infantry and continued the fight in grim and desperate street battles. "We set up on street corners, fired our 155s point-blank at the North Korean tanks. . . . We'd fire into some tanks, then move and set up again two or three blocks away. We did this most of the day,"[41] remembers Corporal Therman Cossairt Jr.

Despite intense fighting, the Americans were pushed back, and more than a thousand were killed, wounded, or missing at the end of the battle. "Sitting here in 1985, I can close my eyes and visualize

U.S. Marines engage in an intense street battle during the initial stages of the Korean conflict. These early skirmishes proved disastrous for American troops.

perfectly what happened that day in Taejon," recalled infantryman Robert Harper. "I can feel my heart beginning to pound. Hard to explain my feelings. Unless you were in Taejon and saw what was happening it would be difficult to understand the emotions."[42]

Shaken by such hard fighting, some soldiers panicked; like Task Force Smith, they sometimes turned and fled, exhibiting what came to be called "bugout fever." This was a derisive term for unauthorized retreats during which fleeing soldiers left rocket launchers, mortars, machine guns, and even wounded buddies behind.

Although men who "bugged out" were condemned as cowards, panic was perhaps the normal reaction to disorganized conditions in the field. Unaware of the overall strategy, at times led by inexperienced officers, and forced to watch their comrades fall all around them, many thought they too would be killed. "On my level, the troop level, there wasn't any sense of a coherent strategy. It seemed like we were continually falling back, and there was no indication where it would end. There was a real fear that we'd be pushed right out of Korea,"[43] says Lieutenant Uzal Ent of the Twenty-fifth Division.

Too Much to Endure

Ordinary soldiers were not the only ones to yield to their emotions during this time. On July 19, 1950, Major General William F. Dean, a decorated World War II veteran, led his men in a determined stand against the North Koreans in Taejon. Rather than direct the fighting from a protected place, Dean surprised everyone by rushing out into the streets on the second day of the battle and fighting alongside ordinary infantrymen. He even went on an extremely risky tank hunt with a bazooka team.

Despite such death-defying behavior, his efforts proved worthless. The Americans were forced to shoot their way out of town; Dean became separated from his men and was captured. Released in September 1953, he remembers his actions in Taejon with embarrassment: "Some people who escaped from Taejon that day

Bugging Out

Lieutenant Colonel Charles Bussey was commander of the Seventy-seventh Engineer Combat Company in Korea. In an interview with CNN, which can be accessed on the news network's website, he points out that "bugout fever" in the Korean War was more often a result of poor leadership than of a lack of courage.

On Battle Mountain, the 24th Infantry won and lost that mountain 19 times. When they left it units that were not under pressure came up with the term "bug out," meaning that you left your position. . . . "Bug out" to me meant just that—that you had left your position and the enemy had taken it over. The fact that you went back the next day and took it *back* over was meaningless. But this did happen. It happened again, [due to] lack of leadership. If your battalion commander's up there and you can hear his voice over the fire and whatnot, you know that he's *there* and that you had better be there too. If you don't hear any voice because he has abandoned you, then troops are subject to bug out. . . . Whether it's a voice over guns or whatever, or you've got to see him, but you've gotta know that he *is there*. We didn't have that and we had occasions when our positions were lost and they were lost because the guy who should've been there wasn't there or he was hunkered down some place, hiding, but he wasn't up there doing his job.

reported they last had seen me firing a pistol at a tank. Well, they did, but I'm not proud of it. As that last tank passed I banged away at it with a .45, but even then I wasn't silly enough to think I could do anything with a pistol. It was plain rage and frustration."[44]

Fighting Buddies

In addition to dealing with frustration on the fighting field, regularly men faced the tensions of working and living in a fighting unit. Although at first glance becoming part of the group seemed like a mundane concern, it was often a serious source of strain.

In the beginning, some fighting units were made up of men who had been together for a period of months. They knew each other, knew their leaders, and had friends whom they relied on and trusted. Lieutenant Adrian B. Brian recalls: "I became very close to two of my men. . . . We used to sit next to our pup tents at night and talk for hours about all topics imaginable. . . . I used to think it was not right for me to like these two so much. I was afraid it would compromise my leadership role or result in my playing favorites, but it never did."[45]

As time passed and men were killed or wounded, or returned home, new men were inserted into old units. Tension was unavoidable as the newcomer and the veteran adjusted to and got to know each other. Neither knew the character, outlook, or past experiences of the other.

Neither knew if the other would be selfless or selfish in a tight situation. Second Lieutenant Tom Gibson remembers his experience as a newcomer to a World War II unit and believes it applies to soldiers everywhere:

> The tough part is knowing that no matter how well you produce, in the minds of the veterans, you're not worth a shit because you could never be as good as Sergeant Jones, Lieutenant Smith, or whoever it is you're replacing. You're unproven, the unknown quantity, and it's tough to trust your life to someone who hasn't earned that trust.[46]

James Brady was one of the untested men assigned to be a replacement in an existing unit. Like many newcomers, he felt deep regard for those who were there before him. Intimidated, his immediate approach was to remain in the background, not ask questions, and respect their privacy. Soon, however, his comfort level rose: "For the first few minutes, I was in awe of them, their combat experience and their wounds. . . . But the longer we marched the less vivid was the difference between us. . . . They were just marines, marines here before me who had been in the fighting, but nothing more. I started to feel better about it, less defensive."[47]

Brady's restraint was wise. The loss of a man from a unit, especially if he had been killed, could be deeply traumatic to those who were left behind. These men

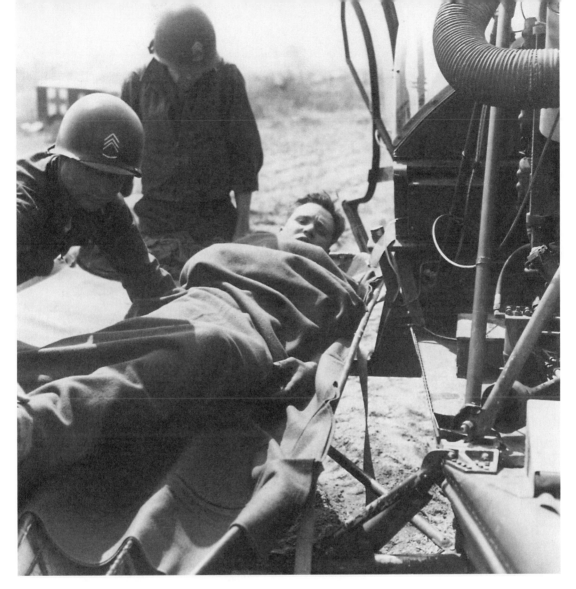

A wounded American soldier is lifted into a helicopter for evacuation. Losing a member of a fighting unit was difficult for those left behind.

usually had no time to examine their emotions or mourn their loss. Instead, they hid their true feelings from newcomers and often reacted by being aloof and guarded rather than welcoming. As marine private Doug Koch observed,

> There was a lot of commotion, caused by the replacements who were coming in to fill the spots left open by the men we'd lost. . . . As I had lost my whole fire team . . . I got three new kids. Although we were together about two weeks, I have to admit I can't remember their names. Maybe this is one way you start to protect yourself; you don't get friendly with people.[48]

Not all veterans were unfriendly, however. Captain Francis "Ike" Fenton Jr. was a member of one of the veteran units that did its best to make newcomers feel comfortable and informed: "We spent four hours every morning conditioning and whipping the men into shape. The old-timers—the combat veterans—of the company deserved a rest, but they dug right in and did their utmost to help these new men feel at home and work together as a unit."[49]

A Larger Struggle

In their trial by fire, American troops soon learned what was expected of them when it came to fighting. They learned the ways of the enemy and developed a tough fighting spirit that carried them through the most depressing days of the

conflict. Not only was the invasion at Inchon successful, but, beginning in September, soldiers began pushing the enemy back toward North Korea. American forces retook Seoul on September 27, 1950. Within weeks, North Korean forces had retreated beyond the 38th parallel.

The United States and its UN allies had achieved the goals that had been set at the beginning of the war—to force the North Korean army to withdraw from South Korea and to restore peace and security in the south. Poised on the 38th parallel with their fighting forces geared up and on the move, however, the temptation to invade North Korea and reunite the country was too strong to resist. It would be a chance to triumph over the Communists. South Korean president Rhee supported the offensive as well.

The Value of Experience

The presence of World War II veterans in the Korean War was invaluable for those men who were new to the military and inclined to panic under fire. In Donald Knox's oral history, *The Korean War: Pusan to Chosin*, Private Doug Koch cites the case of Gunny Reeves, who had served twenty-nine years in the Marine Corps and was not rattled by anything.

When we drove through [the town of] Masan it was dark and very eerie. I was twenty years old. Except for the officers and staff NCOs [noncommissioned officers], most of us were kids—eighteen-, nineteen-, twenty-year-olds. No doubt we were gung ho [enthusiastic]. We thought we were

pretty tough, too. Underneath, though, we were pretty scared. Anyone who says he wasn't is lying.

West of Masan, in the distance, I could hear artillery. Then, not more than 100 yards away, an enemy shell exploded! Right then and there we kids were ready to bail out of the truck and hit the ditch. Old Gunny [Harold] Reeves stood up and growled, " . . . Set your ass down. By God, when you see me getting nervous and excited, that's the time to really get nervous and excited." We sat back down. The gunnery sergeant settled us kids right down. The truck went up the road a little farther and about daylight we unloaded.

Thus, on September 27, 1950, the Joint Chiefs of Staff of the U.S. armed forces authorized General MacArthur to carry the war northward.

American soldiers in Korea suddenly found themselves committed to a much larger struggle. Private Leonard Korgie remembers:

> Our dreams of a short war were shattered the morning of October 9 when

U.S. infantrymen of the First Cavalry Division march northward to the 38th parallel.

we were awakened by the clank of tanks and the roar of trucks. What the hell was this?! We learned the boys in the 1st Cav [Cavalry] were crossing the [38th] Parallel. We were told we were going to cross, too. No one knew why or how far we would go.[50]

Chapter 3

To the Yalu and Back

Despite initial confusion, the victories of September 1950 lifted soldiers' spirits, and most were eager to move northward. One man expressed the assurance of many when he said, "The company felt good about itself. We were veterans now, and very confident. We'd kicked the shit out of the North Koreans. . . . If we worried at all, it was wondering whether the Navy could get the next job done, and get us in, wherever that would be."[51]

The days ahead would test that confidence, full of hard fighting and difficulties that ranged from sore feet to attacks from thousands of angry Chinese. James Cardinal wrote in a letter home, "Believe me, sleeping in foxholes in a drizzling rain, cold and waiting to attack, dodging bullets, and going for three or four days with one small meal is not as romantic as the movies make out. I'm glad I've gone through the experience but believe me, never again."[52]

Street Fighting

With a new goal before them, U.S. fighting men focused on their assigned objectives. At times, that involved capturing villages and cities. Many had already gone through desperate street fighting in Seoul in early September, with snipers and roadblocks making progress slow and dangerous. "I can remember going down this street and coming to an intersection. Later, we called it Blood and Bones Corner. At first it didn't seem different. One of our fire teams made it across without problems. It was when the next team tried to cross that all hell broke loose,"[53] says marine private Jack Wright. The city was declared liberated from the Communists on September 27, but it took another three days of fighting to clear out enemy resistance.

Ironically, capturing Pyongyang, the capital of North Korea, on October 19, 1950, proved less difficult. Heavy bombing had softened resistance, the North Korean government had fled, and Americans were able to enter with little hard fighting. Private Victor Fox remembers, "In the afternoon we cleared the downtown and business sectors. . . . There was the expected sniper and occasional harassing fire but nothing in the way of all-out street-to-street, door-to-door fighting that had gone on in Seoul."[54]

Taking the town of Chipyong-ni on February 12, 1951, involved a savage five-day battle. UN soldiers were cut off from reinforcements, ran low of ammunition, and had to resort to close-range combat to stay alive. Joe Sammarco, a forward observer and liaison sergeant, described the toughness of the battle in a letter to his wife: "There were 4 divisions of Chinese around us, and the last two nights they broke through our lines and we were fighting hand to hand in the streets & houses. . . . Several times I thought it was all over for me, but I was lucky."[55]

The Americans eventually won the battle, with enemy losses estimated to be between two thousand and five thousand dead. Victor Fox describes the scene afterward: "I saw the bodies of hundreds of Chinese piled in grisly heaps. Everywhere I looked were these mounds of frozen Chinese bodies lying every which way in their mustard-colored quilted uniforms. . . . I never saw such carnage."[56]

Taxed to the Limit

Although U.S. forces saw some city battles, both North and South Korea were largely rural, so the bulk of the fighting took place in fields and in the rugged hills that dominated the landscape. This was unfamiliar terrain to American soldiers, but they soon became used to wading through flooded rice paddies, clambering up rocky slopes, and skidding down brushy embankments. Gaining control of a piece of

Horrors of War

Some soldiers witnessed the horrors of war during the battle to liberate Seoul, the South Korean capital. In Donald Knox's *The Korean War: Pusan to Chosin*, marine sergeant Lee Bergee described some unforgettable sights in the hot, smoky city in late September 1950.

As we fought yard by yard up Ma-Po Boulevard, tanks led the way. I saw a North Korean soldier lying in the street. He'd been hit by a burst of white phosphorus. His body was still burning. I watched one of the tanks roll over him, crushing and grinding his body into the pavement. During this period our battalion lost four ambulances; seven corpsmen [navy paramedics] and four drivers were killed.

I remember one day during "[General Edward M.] Almond's mopping up" when our battalion gained exactly 1,200 yards. At each barricade we had to annihilate the enemy, then reorganize, evacuate casualties, and wearily go on to the next. At the railroad station we found the still-warm bodies of women and children—hostages massacred by the North Korean secret police.

high ground was always a tactical advantage, because it is easier to see and fire down on the enemy from higher elevations. Nevertheless, there were times when getting to the crest of a hill was a triumph. "We finally reached the summit of a very difficult, tortuous ridge which we had climbed on our hands and knees, holding onto roots to keep from sliding back down the trail,"[57] remembers marine lieutenant colonel Raymond Davis.

Fatigue was an enemy of all soldiers. Hiking on uneven ground was enormously tiring, and climbing hills while carrying weapons and knapsacks that weighed sixty pounds or more added to the strain. Sleep was often interrupted by all-night firefights. Battles lasted for days at a time, and men who were fighting and moving constantly found their physical reserves were taxed to the limit. While on a search patrol, John Sullivan describes a moment when he was literally too tired to stand:

When I tried to stand, my legs gave way beneath me. Try as I might, I just couldn't get them to function. There

U.S. Marines carry heavy knapsacks and weaponry as they hike along a winding mountain road. Marching on uneven terrain with such loads was extremely fatiguing.

was no pain, or any feeling. . . . Seeing the gun crew getting farther and farther ahead of me, I made a last effort and managed to move about ten yards before falling to the ground. I thought I might have been hit in the legs, but could see no blood."[58]

The adrenaline rush of battle allowed soldiers to overcome their fatigue, but when it was over, they collapsed, sometimes exhibiting what was known as "the thousand-yard stare," a profoundly blank gaze into space that suggested emotional as well as physical overload. In many cases, men became so tired that they took extraordinary risks, as war correspondent Harold Martin notes: "The infantry moved out. They went in long, thinly spaced files across the emerald rice paddies, walking upright despite the sniper fire, for in war men sometimes grow so weary they do not give a damn whether they live or die, and these men were going into battle tired."[59]

Booby Traps

Despite their fatigue, soldiers needed to be alert at all times, especially when land mines and booby traps were everywhere. Tens of thousands of soldiers on both sides were killed or injured in the war by these hidden dangers.

American forces were the first to use land mines, some of which were designed as antitank weapons and were commonly placed on roads where tanks would roll.

Antipersonnel mines, designed to kill humans, were also used, however, and the enemy frequently used them in creative ways. For instance, they set up roadblocks made of fallen trees or piles of branches with a mine attached underneath. When soldiers moved the obstruction, they detonated the explosive. Cars, tanks, corpses, radios, flashlights, and other objects that might be picked up were also booby-trapped with disastrous effect.

Americans sometimes sabotaged themselves by sowing land mines in a field or on a hillside without recording where they had planted them. If they later returned across that ground, they became victims of their own carelessness. Colonel David C. Hackworth remembers an incident in 1952, when as a lieutenant he was ordered to clear a path through one such unmapped territory: "I argued with my colonel about the smarts of doing such work on snow-covered ground. Lieutenants seldom win disputes with colonels, so the mine-clearing detail proceeded as ordered until a young kid named Simmons tripped the wire on a "Bouncing Betty" mine. It popped up from the ground and blew off the top of his head, covering me with his blood and brains. . . . Then, only then, was the mine-clearing project cancelled."[60]

"The Miseries of War"

Aside from the stresses of land mines and booby traps, extremes of the climate made fighting difficult. In August, when

Danger: Land Mines

Land mines in Korea originated from two main sources, the United States and the Soviet Union. In *The Outpost War: U.S. Marines in Korea*, author Lee Ballenger describes two common mines and how they functioned.

The most commonly found Soviet mine was the Schu mine, consisting of a crudely constructed wooden box, about half the size of a cigar box, with a hinged lid. The explosive charge was a three-eighth pound block of TNT. . . . This weapon required only two pounds of weight to detonate and contained no metal to register on a mine detector. Buried in a path or a road edge, it instantly ended the war for an unsuspecting infantryman.

The American antipersonnel mine, called Bouncing Betty, was particularly insidious [dangerous]. When triggered, often by trip wire, it sprang from the ground and exploded at waist height. . . . Instead of taking a foot or leg, as did the Schu, the Bouncing Betty targeted bigger body parts, such as the abdomen, and was most effective in taking the victim out of action, usually forever.

the first men arrived, high humidity and temperatures over one hundred degrees Fahrenheit left many suffering from heat exhaustion. Captain Joseph Fegan recalls, "The heat was vicious. . . . We were constantly wet with sweat. The company had the lead one day and I became particularly concerned because so many men were dropping from heat prostration."[61]

During the hot season lack of water also drove many men to desperation. Un-aware that they would not be able find a clean water source to refill their canteens, they often drank all they had, then suffered agonies of thirst. "Guys almost went mad for water. I never felt the kind of heat I felt in Korea. I just burned up. My hands went numb. I couldn't help myself; I began crying like a baby,"[62] says serviceman Jack Wright. Many men took a chance and drank unsterilized water from the rice paddies they crossed, and then became seriously ill from the bacteria that polluted it.

While days were hot, nights could be chilly, and the monsoon season brought torrents of drenching rain. Captain Norman Allen wrote home, "All the miseries of war have been present the last three days. Boiling sun by day, cold rain at night, trying to sleep sitting in a foxhole with four inches of water in it, . . . wet clear to the bone, sand in our weapons and cartridge clips."[63]

The hot, wet environment led to fungus infections, the most serious of which was trenchfoot. Prolonged exposure to moisture caused the skin of the feet to soften and become red, swollen, and infected. Often skin would peel or slough off. Serious cases sometimes required amputation, so men were constantly reminded to change their socks and keep their feet dry. This was almost impossible because they lived outdoors and were often walking through water, so many men suffered. After a time, newly developed vapor barrier socks and insulated boots were issued and helped reduce foot problems.

Dangerous Cold

Winters in Korea were as cold as summers were hot. The winter of 1950–1951 set records for low temperatures, and men in the field suffered constantly, especially when everything was covered with a chill blanket of snow. Men already worrying about trenchfoot now also had to try to avoid frostbite, which was as serious and prevalent as battle wounds. Toes could freeze solid in a short period of time, and prevention was nearly impossible because there were very few places one could go to get warm. Many men lived with the condition until they could get to the rear and seek medical attention. War correspondent N. Harry Smith writes:

Troops had to contend with snow and freezing temperatures during Korea's harsh winter months.

I noticed that many of the men walked with a peculiar gait resembling men treading barefoot across a plank studded with spikes. They looked like light-footed marionettes; they kept bounding off the balls of their feet. These Marines were walking upon frostbitten feet and had refused to turn themselves in to the doctor for fear of being evacuated by air as so many of them had been. Others were too proud to complain. Their pride kept them in the designated category of "walking casualties."[64]

In the intense cold, feet were not the only things to freeze. Food had to be chipped out of cans. Water froze in canteens. The ground froze, making it impossible to dig foxholes. Men could not light frozen fuses and had to put their rifles inside their clothes to keep the firing pins from freezing. When that technique failed, they sometimes resorted to more unconventional tactics, as Tony Herbert describes: "Our weapons were frozen. Firing pins immovable. 'Piss on them,' someone said, and word came down the line. We pissed on them and it worked. The urine melted the ice, and troops all along the line began to fire."[65]

Dirt and Discomfort

Military handbooks taught more conventional survival techniques; in Korea their advice was sometimes impractical. For instance, guidelines that encouraged soldiers to avoid fungus infections by washing with soap and warm water regularly were treated as a joke. Cleanliness was an almost nonexistent luxury for combat troops in Korea. The military tried to provide portable bathing facilities so that everyone could shower every five days or so, but some men went weeks without washing themselves or their clothes. Sweat, dust, and smoke coated them in hot weather. Mud caked them in rainy, snowy seasons.

In addition to the dirt, infestations of fleas and lice were a constant problem. "The lice dug into my skin like peanuts in a shell. When I got warm, my body itched terribly. I scratched and scratched until I bled,"[66] remembers one veteran. DDT, a powdered insecticide, was usually distributed when lice became too great a problem, but because of the prevalence of

Soldiers in Korea struggled to stay clean and free from parasites like this head louse.

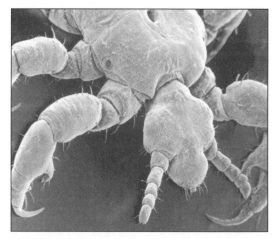

such pests, infestations reappeared and men had to be treated repeatedly.

Most men took advantage of every opportunity to clean up. They bathed in rivers and streams, heated water in their helmets over open fires to shave, and washed their faces in snow when nothing else was available. At times, they hired cooperative South Korean women to launder their uniforms. These women could be unreliable however, as marine captain Joseph Fegan discovered: "When [my clothes] dried they were stiff as cardboard. . . . Apparently my Korean laundress didn't use strong enough soap. On the road the next day, my gunnery sergeant, Ray Morgan, said to me, 'Skipper, I hate to tell you this, but you still stink!' And I did."[67]

In addition to dirty clothing, shortages of shoes, trousers, socks, and even toothbrushes at various times left men ragged and uncomfortable. A lack of warm winter uniforms and heavy sleeping bags was a big problem when temperatures dropped in the fall of 1950. Sergeant Warren Avery notes:

> We had not been issued any winter equipment. . . . All each GI had was a poncho and a blanket. To keep warm, three of us would place two ponchos on the frozen ground to lie on. Then we'd cover ourselves with the three blankets and the remaining poncho. This way we got a fairly comfortable sleep.[68]

After a time, warmer clothes and cold weather sleeping bags were issued. Most men eventually wore heavy gloves, a heavy hooded jacket, and long underwear as well. While these did not totally ease their discomfort, it kept most of them alive.

Chow in a Can

American soldiers insisted that bad food was another hardship of the war, but in fact all were better fed than North Koreans or Communist Chinese, who sometimes subsisted only on a daily portion of rice. All U.S. troops were issued army C rations (canned food), which included a variety of entrees such as spaghetti, meat and noodles, or chicken and vegetables. Though C rations had an overcooked texture and a monotonous flavor, they were nourishing and could readily be heated. Everyone had their favorites. Private Ernest Gonzalez notes, "We roamed in groups looking for certain types of food. My favorite was wieners and beans. I didn't find any. My least favorite was pork and lima beans. I found plenty of those."[69]

At times, supply lines were cut off and soldiers did suffer from a lack of food. James Cardinal remembers that near the North Korean capital of Pyongyang, a typical meal was a slice of Spam (processed meat) and half a cup of grapefruit juice once a day. As the men grew hungrier, they spent time dreaming about favorite foods they had enjoyed at home—roast turkey, homemade pie, ice cream, and the like. Cardinal notes, "This is when I

The Army's Greatest Invention

In *Korean Vignettes: Faces of War*, Paul A. Free-burger recalls one of the smallest pieces of military equipment in war—a 1.5-inch rectangular piece of metal with a swing-out blade, designed to open C-ration cans. He details its value in the following excerpt.

It was developed in just 30 days in the summer of 1942 by the Subsistence Board Laboratory in Chicago. Never in its 55 year history has it been known to break, rust, need sharpening or polishing. It is for those reasons that soldiers, past and present, have come to regard the P-38 C-Ration can opener as one of the greatest of Army inventions. It has had a multitude of names: the P-38, the Church Key, DogTag Bracelet, Bride's Best Friend, 10-in-one opener, to name a few. . . .

The P-38 opened cans, but it did so much more. Any soldier will tell you that. Hung around his neck, it became a part of him. He was never without it.

[Uses for P-38:] Seam Ripper . . . Screwdriver . . . Clean Fingernails . . . Cut fishing line . . . Open paint cans . . . Window scraper . . . Clean floor corners . . . Clean out small cracks . . . Scrape boots . . . Bottle opener . . . Test for doneness on camp fire . . . Prying small objects . . . Toothpick . . . Measuring . . . Striking flint . . . Send Morse code . . . Box cutter . . . Letter opener . . . Scratch an itch . . . Rip off chevrons for field promotions/demotions . . . Field strip and clean weapons . . . Paper cutter . . . Carburetor adjustment tool . . . Knife . . . War service souvenir.

became very fond of lamb, a meat my mother never used to serve in our home. An Armenian American in the Second Platoon talked of nothing but lamb: roasted, broiled, baked, on rice, with potatoes, smothered in herbs—lamb, lamb, lamb."[70]

In contrast, on occasion soldiers were served meals that almost measured up to "Mom's home cooking." Such special efforts were usually made on holidays, after a battle, or during a lull in the fighting, when kitchen units and cooks could move up and prepare hot meals on the spot. Depending on the time and place, menus ranged from full Thanksgiving dinners to pancakes and steak. James Brady remembers, "It didn't really matter what the food

was, or how it tasted. It was hot and it was different and you didn't have to use a can opener to get at it. We rarely had bread. Fresh bread, you learned the value of bread, and promised yourself you would never again take it for granted."[71]

Enter the Chinese

Despite complaints, many soldiers were willing to put up with all kinds of hardships in the fall of 1950 as they swept through North Korea. The war was going their way, and a victorious end seemed in sight. By November 1 some U.S. troops were only eighteen miles from the Yalu River, on the other side of which lay China. MacArthur announced on November 24 that everyone would be home for Christmas. "It was at this time that everyone, including our commanders, thought the war was over. To reach the Yalu all you had to do was get on the road and drive north until you got wet,"[72] says Lacy Barnett.

Their optimism was misplaced. Leaders of Communist China had repeatedly warned the United States that they would not tolerate an invasion of North Korea. Their primary concern was that U.S. troops might not stop at the Yalu River and might decide to invade mainland China. MacArthur's hints that he would support an invasion of China increased their antagonism. Thus, as American forces moved northward in mid-October, the first Communist Chinese forces (CCF) began moving into North Korea to join in the fighting.

At first MacArthur and other military leaders denied that the Chinese had entered the war. American soldiers knew otherwise. They had seen Chinese prisoners and Chinese dead in distinctive, light-colored quilted uniforms. "Our intelligence reports had been telling us they were in the area. We were well aware that the border was only fifty miles away. But the intentions of these Chinese were by no means clear to us,"[73] observes Sherman Pratt, a veteran of both World War II and Korea.

The CCF's objectives became clear as over three hundred thousand Chinese troops swooped down on MacArthur's forces. Their numbers were simply overwhelming. After battling fiercely to hold their ground, parts of the Eighth Army were virtually destroyed and had to retreat. X Corps, which had been advancing in eastern North Korea, had to do the same.

Frozen Chosin

During the U.S. withdrawal from North Korea, one of the most unforgettable battles of the war took place. In the mountains near the Chosin (or Changjin Reservoir) in late November 1950, X Corps was surrounded by thousands of Chinese. N. Harry Smith, who was with the marines, describes the scene: "Out of the hills to the northwest poured hundreds of Chinese soldiers. Like ants running toward a drop of honey, they came shouting, shooting rifles and burp guns, crawling on their stomachs, stumbling, running."[74]

The Americans fought hard for days. Snow and bitterly cold temperatures added to their misery. Large numbers of men were lost on both sides. One of the survivors, Private Bob Hammond, later wrote to his parents, "They were on all sides of us and we were masecured [massacred].... Out of 1,400 men we had, just 400 got back. A Battery had 180 men. We now have 42. 32 are wounded."[75]

Surrounded on all sides by superior forces, X Corps had no easy retreat. Instead they had to "break out"—that is, fight their way to safety. "It was a battle all the way. The frost and wind, howling through the narrow pass, were almost as deadly as the enemy. Bumper to bumper, trucks, half-tracks, and bulldozers slipped and scraped down the mountain. Mortars lobbed in, and sometimes the convoy had to stop for hours while engineers filled in the holes,"[76] reports war correspondent Marguerite Higgins.

Hundreds died in the fight to escape. Others were close to collapse when they were rescued. Private James Ransone Jr., who was among those who crossed the frozen reservoir to get away, remembers, "I was disoriented, exhausted, nearly frozen, hungry, and vomiting blood. The temperature at night was 20 or more degrees below zero. The wind was so strong it was hard to stand or walk on the ice. In the early morning hours, my group ran into a Marine outpost at the southern end of the Chosin Reservoir."[77]

At the end of the engagement, which many veterans still refer to as "Frozen Chosin," almost forty thousand North Korean and Communist Chinese were dead or wounded. About twenty-five hundred U.S. and ROK men had been killed in action, five thousand had been wounded, and seventy-five hundred suffered from frostbite and other cold-related injuries. Jack Wright describes the extent of the losses in more personal terms: "[My company sergeant] told me where I would find my platoon area. I hobbled down there, but didn't see anyone I knew. That afternoon they called a muster [roll call]. Third Platoon fell in, all three of us."[78] (A platoon usually consists of fifteen to forty-eight men).

"We Dug In"

After the Battle of Chosin Reservoir and the entry of the Chinese into Korea, the fortunes of war changed. U.S. troops

A U.S. Marine at the Chosin Reservoir lies covered with ice and snow. During the two-week battle, temperatures plummeted to thirty degrees below zero.

A group of U.S. Marines evacuates an injured soldier down a snowy mountain road near the Chosin Reservoir.

were relentlessly pushed south. They abandoned Pyongyang on December 5 and recrossed the 38th parallel about December 15. Seoul once again fell to the Communists on January 3, 1951. Matthew Ridgway, who took over the Eighth Army after the death of General Walton Walker on December 23, 1950, finally stabilized his forces along the 37th parallel on January 14, 1951. The withdrawal from North Korea covered about three hundred miles and went down as one of the longest retreats in military history.

Used to the fortunes of war, Ridgway did not let the losses stop him. He believed that, with so many good men in his fighting force, the defeats of the past month could be reversed. Nevertheless, he realized that morale was again low: "Before going on the offensive, we had work to do, weaknesses to shore up, mis-

takes to learn from, faulty procedures to correct, and a sense of pride to restore."[79]

Ridgway's good leadership soon helped rebuild the men's self-esteem. On July 10, 1951, however, the beginning of peace talks stalled a new offensive. Soldiers who had formerly been constantly on the move were soon entrenched along the 38th parallel, waiting to see what would happen. James Brady remembers, "By November of 1951 there was no more oratory. . . . The Chinese, a million of them, and what was left of the North Koreans dug in. And we dug in, six American divisions and our UN allies. Two armies stood and faced each other in the hills with another damned winter coming out of Siberia."[80]

Chapter 4

Fighting the Bunker War

With peace talks under way, the war became a series of fierce battles along a heavily fortified line of defense known as the Main Line of Resistance (MLR). This front angled from forty miles north of the 38th parallel in the east to a few miles below it in the west. Along it, men tried to survive heavy shelling and hard offensives designed to capture a hill or another few miles of land. Private Doug Michaud notes:

> This part of the war got very confusing. It was just one hill battle after another. You take a hill, and they try to take it back. . . . You'd take a hill, but then there was another one to take. . . . We were very busy—marching, plugging gaps, climbing hills, fighting battles . . . keeping our heads down— very, very busy. But we really weren't accomplishing anything.[81]

Living Underground

The hills, the heat, the cold, and the dirt remained the same during the second and third years of the war, as units positioned their artillery to pound the enemy facing them just a few hills away. Men commonly dug in on a rear slope, where they were moderately protected from direct artillery fire. All quickly learned that to show oneself at the top of a ridgeline meant almost certain death. Even peering over the top using a pair of binoculars was dangerous, because lenses could reflect light, making an easy target for snipers.

Bunkers—shelters in which men lived —were built by tunneling about eight feet into the hill, then hollowing out a cave-like room about twelve feet by twelve feet at the end of the tunnel. Doors were made of canvas or boards. Ceilings were shored up with wood and logs, and the ground above was covered with sandbags, more logs, and dirt. Corporal Ben Judd's bunker was reinforced with solid rock. He recalls gratefully, "I remember six direct hits on those rocks, and I wondered each time whether they would collapse. My assistant was an old hillbilly from the mountains of

Kentucky who knew how to build log cabin chimneys from rock and stone. He built our bunker well."[82]

The slopes on which units lived and fought were originally covered with evergreen trees and brush, but were soon stripped of all greenery as trees were used for firewood or bunker construction. The bare, exposed earth was muddy when it rained, snow covered in winter, and scarred with stumps and trampled trails at all times.

Crude and Filthy

Bunkers could hold up to six men, and were heated by a small wood or kerosene stove. Bunks inside were made of logs and steel pickets, and were laced with communication wire that was strong enough to hold an air mattress and a sleeping bag. Men covered the dirt floors with straw mats and used ammunition boxes for tables, candles or a lantern for light.

Although bunkers offered protection from the rain, snow, and wind, they were filthy residences, usually smelling strongly of dirty bodies and kerosene. "We lived in crude bunkers of sandbags and logs, and when we coughed, it came up black as soot. During shellings or thaws, bunkers collapsed and buried men alive,"[83] says James Brady.

U.S. infantrymen take cover in an underground bunker during a battle at Heartbreak Ridge.

Bathroom facilities were usually a trench some distance away from camp, and during cold or wet weather, a pipe stuck into the ground outside each bunker served as a make-do toilet. Men regularly threw their trash, ration cans, and scrap papers outside their doors, and the litter attracted rats, mice, and other vermin looking for warmth and food. Herb Renner remembers:

When on the bunk reading, rats in the overhead logs read along with you and helped themselves to the chow. We had a mutual understanding. Stay off our face when we were sleeping and we won't throw a concussion grenade in the bunker to kill you. I swear to this day that Korean rats could read English and loved their gourmet C-rations.[84]

Patrols in the Night

Rats were not the only nighttime dangers. The enemy preferred to attack under cover of darkness, sometimes sending mortars flying across the sky, sometimes sending in suicide fighters for hand-to-hand combat. Thus, defense perimeters were set up, made of rolls of barbed wire and mine-

Heavy Loads

When moving from one camp to another or when going out on a lengthy patrol in winter, men carried as much as 150 pounds of clothing and equipment. Veteran and author John A. Sullivan explains exactly what that included in his book, *Toy Soldiers: Memoir of a Combat Platoon Leader in Korea.*

The clothing alone was a heavy load. The GIs wore the usual socks, underwear, fatigue pants and jacket, thermal boots, field pants and jacket, and gloves. A heavy steel helmet and fiber helmet liner rested atop a wool-lined fatigue cap on each head, while a heavier armored vest was worn between the fatigue jacket and the field jacket. . . .

There was a field pack with extra socks, underwear, ration cans, and whatever personal items desired. Around the sides and top of this pack was draped a roll containing a shelter-half [one-half of a pup tent] blanket, and tent poles and rope. On top of this roll was a rolled-up sleeping bag and parka. And strapped to the back of the pack was the . . . entrenching tool. All this was lashed to a cargo pack frame. . . .

A cartridge belt was included to sort of hold everything together. And, so as not to waste such a versatile piece of gear, a variety of items was suspended from same. Thus a canteen, bayonet, and first-aid packet were attached to everyone; a compass, .45 automatic and holster, and two clips of .45 ammo [ammunition] could be added to the belts of those in need of such . . . mine included.

Almost as an afterthought the Army provided each man a basic weapon. For most it was the M-1 rifle. . . . And, of course, with each weapon came the basic load of ammo. . . . Field jacket pockets were stuffed with at least six hand grenades and a few emergency clips or magazines of ammo.

fields. Guards were posted, and some units hung empty ammunition cans or other types of booby traps on the wire, hoping that they would create noise if the enemy bumped into them while sneaking close.

Patrols were also sent out at night for reasons of practicality. James Brady explains: "The artillery on both sides was too good, too deadly by day, and so we fought by night—creeping out through the barbed wire and the mine fields with grenades and automatic weapons, with shotguns and knives, to lie shivering in the snow, waiting in ambush."[85]

There were three types of patrols. The first was ambush, during which soldiers lay in wait to kill or capture enemy troops who might be passing by. The second was reconnaissance (recon), where men explored a region to get information on the enemy. The third was combat, during which battle was joined. All patrols were dangerous, but some men preferred one kind over another. Herb Renner remembers:

I liked the ambush patrol in the spring because we could lay out under the stars and wait for the gooks [Chinese or North Koreans] to find us (which they seldom did.) In winter the recon patrols were the best, you could keep warm moving around. Combat patrols involved getting into the gooks' trenches and blowing up their outpost bunkers. These weren't fun, because the gooks would get mad as hell and fight back.[86]

On patrol, men usually walked stealthily in a line or V position, and the most dangerous place to be was "on point"—the lead man of the group. The point man was responsible for scanning the ground and detecting danger ahead, a charge that was extremely stressful and usually exhausting. Being on point carried a high risk of personal injury, and was a strictly volunteer arrangement. Author and veteran Martin Russ notes, "Unless he [the point man] is completely alert, he is the one who will lead the others into an ambush, and he will be the one who steps on a land mine or tripwire."[87]

The man in the rear of a patrol also held a position of responsibility, because he guarded the others from an attack from the rear. This usually meant that he walked backwards at least part of the time and made a relatively easy target, as Corporal Clarence Burrill remembers: "The Chinese loved to snatch the last man on a patrol without alerting the others. We had heard of a number of such cases where this had happened."[88]

Hill Fights

No matter what their assignment, men on the front lines took part in many bloody battles as they fought to push back the enemy or capture a ridge or a valley that had some strategic value. Often battles centered around hills that were known only by their height in meters above sea level—Hill 191, Hill 383, Hill 717. Sometimes the hills were nicknamed for their

shape—Old Baldy, Pork Chop Hill, and Horseshoe Ridge, for example—or for the military outposts located on them—Vegas, Carson, Reno, Berlin, and East Berlin.

Some of the toughest battles took place in or near the so-called Punchbowl, an ancient volcanic crater in eastern Korea, four or five miles in diameter. One of its sections was nicknamed "Bloody Ridge" for the intensity of the fighting that took place there in August 1951.

On Bloody Ridge, the North Koreans occupied the high ground, allowing them to pour machine-gun fire and hand

Soldiers on the front lines fought in bloody battles to take control of strategically important ridges and valleys.

grenades down on Allied positions and roads to the south. American forces were determined to dislodge them. "There were many firefights, all too painful to recall in particular or detail. The hill was attacked continuously,"[89] remembers Ben Judd.

The Americans finally captured the ridge on September 6, 1951, after a month of fighting. The North Koreans had lost an estimated fifteen thousand soldiers. U.S. and South Korean casualties numbered twenty-seven hundred. Years after the war, Sherman Pratt thought back on those casualties: "I could see men trying to get the wounded off the slopes. Taking out the wounded was always a problem in these hill fights. It often took three or four men to get one wounded man down off the hill and if you've got twenty or thirty wounded at a time, which was not at all uncommon, you had a lot of men who weren't doing any fighting."[90] On September 13, almost immediately after Bloody Ridge, the battle for nearby Heartbreak Ridge began. Again, a well-entrenched enemy was able to rain artillery on U.S. troops. "Shells fell over the

entire company. There was no place they were not falling, and there was no place to take cover. We sat like ducks in a hailstorm of fire,"[91] recalls Judd.

The fight for the ridge lasted another month, with both sides hotly contesting the heights, sometimes several times a day. "The hills and the fighting just went on and on and on. One hill we eventually bypassed—just went around it. It was so steep, we just spun our wheels trying to climb it. . . . I don't know how many

American soldiers carry wounded comrades down from Heartbreak Ridge. The enemy bombarded U.S. troops with artillery during the battle for the ridge.

assaults were staged on that hill. Seemed like every time a unit went up, only half its men came back,"[92] remembers Sergeant Darrald Feaker.

Just as at Bloody Ridge, the battle took a tremendous toll on both men and countryside. An estimated thirty-seven hundred U.S. or UN men were injured or killed, while the Chinese and North Koreans lost an estimated twenty-five thousand men. In the end, the ridge had the appearance of a forest following a sweeping fire, with only bare remains of trees and shrubs showing that once heavy underbrush had covered the sheer slopes.

What's for Dinner?

The effects of so much death and devastation were made worse by the discomforts that men endured while fighting on the front lines. No one expected soap, water, clean clothes, and soft beds, but shortages of food and water, although temporary, seemed unbearable. Seymour "Hoppy" Harris, a gunner with Company H, Twenty-third Infantry Regiment, wrote in a letter to a friend:

> Food was a real problem on Heartbreak. Water was always in short supply, the same with C-rations. They made sure we had ammo. I can't remember ever being short of ammo. But it seemed we were hungry and thirsty most of the time. Once in a while they brought up thermos cans with chow and we'd get a decent meal. But not often. We usually got our meals down on the road [later].[93]

Fortunately, such shortages were unusual. Most men were supplied with plenty of C rations and were usually served two hot meals a day when battles were not blazing. Meals were prepared in bulk and carried up from a mess tent in the rear in insulated Mermite cans. These resembled garbage cans and kept everything from coffee to creamed chipped beef at least moderately warm until the men could eat. Victor Fox notes, "Breakfast was the best time of day because we were all glad to see the light of a new day, and it meant exchanging 'the scoop,' or news, with the mess cooks from the rear."[94]

Food was plentiful and nourishing but tended to be bland, overcooked, and uninteresting. A common meal was an unidentifiable patty dubbed "mystery meat," served with a scoop of lumpy mashed potatoes, canned fruit or vegetables, two slices of white bread, and coffee in a tin cup. Herb Renner says, "Sometimes we could find a mess tent in the rear serving cube steak and powdered eggs with reconstituted milk. The king of all meals."[95]

Routine

Between meals, soldiers used daylight hours to catch up on sleep. Days were also times when the men performed mundane activities such as repairing or strengthening bunkers and defense lines, cleaning their guns, or writing letters

Low Time

Men passed the time in different ways during lulls in the war. In *The Last Parallel*, Korean War veteran Martin Russ notes in his journal that quiet times were not necessarily enjoyable ones.

> Every afternoon I carry a blanket up to an old deserted bunker just behind the MLR and write in this thing. I write until it becomes late afternoon. I loathe late afternoon, and this is so distracting that I stop scribbling as soon as I notice that the shadows are beginning to lengthen. It always makes me think of New York, when the street lights go on and crowds of people leave the office buildings. Late afternoon means that it will soon be time for the patrols to get ready to depart. Only when it becomes totally dark does this uneasy feeling go away or diminish. Late afternoon is the time when the men are at their lowest.

home. Many passed the time playing cards, reading, or talking to one another about what they planned to do when they returned to the United States. "Being right there on the front lines made most talk of the future seem like wistful fantasy, but the men had to believe they were going to leave Korea, and that some day they would have a future somewhere else,"[96] remembers Victor Fox.

Other than those activities, men had few pleasures to lighten their existence. If they were close enough to a village, a few patronized the local bar or prostitutes who were eager to get American dollars.

"If you were looking for a semi-permanent relationship, you could actually buy a young girl of about 14 or so from her parents, for about $100," Seabee mechanic Bob Markey recalls. "The people were very poor and that hundred would buy them a new home, such as it was. I never sank so low as to even consider doing anything like that, but a few of the guys did. It was disgusting."[97]

Men with some musical talent sometimes entertained others by playing a guitar or harmonica or by singing. "I don't know about other units, but Item Company sang a lot," remembers Victor Fox. "Most of it was led by the southern boys. . . . We sang mostly what we called 'hillbilly' songs—the term *country and western* had not been coined yet."[98]

Mail call was a highlight of the day. Letters and hometown newspapers were always appreciated, although accounts of the war in the latter were generally judged inaccurate. Fox observes, "After mail call we read newspaper clippings about the war that parents had sent. It was a different war. Some guy would say, 'What'n hell are they writing about? Where's that war?'"[99]

Some men also had cameras and took pictures when no fighting was going on. Marvin Muskat remembers, "You fought in Korea with guns and with cameras. . . . I have pictures of Heartbreak Ridge that show every foxhole, every trench line, every broken tree stump, every sandbag castle."[100]

War Wounds

In his book *The Coldest War: A Memoir of Korea*, veteran James Brady points out that battle wounds were not the only injuries soldiers had to deal with in Korea.

Men were always getting hurt. I don't mean wounds. Take hands; your knuckles were always chapped and sore and red, cracking and dry. . . . Your lips were always chapped and sore, sometimes so cracked they bled. . . . Getting hurt was something that happened to us every day: twisting an ankle on the ice or smashing a thumb in the bolt of a weapon or cutting your hand on a ration can or chipping a tooth or tearing off a fingernail trying to shore up the ceiling logs or dropping a jerrican [a large, flat can] of water on your foot or bruising your knees or your elbows or your hips just moving around in the dark on a big snow-covered hill laced with wire and pitted with holes and veiny with trenches. There were men with rheumatism from the wet months and sleeping on the ground. . . . And men who had been frostbitten early and had to keep those parts covered the best they could because the tissue was damaged and would always be susceptible afterward. That happened to my ears, both of them, the lobes.

Warming Tents

Snowy winters in Korea could be picture-postcard beautiful, but the cold and wet conditions made everything from patrolling to firing weapons difficult. Men could be easily seen by the enemy against a background of white. Ambush patrols were agony for those who had to lie motionless on the ground for hours at a time. Even going to the toilet was challenging. Men had to unfasten and lower multiple layers of clothing, exposing their bodies to subzero temperatures, then try to refasten everything with fingers that were stiff and numb.

Aware that the cold could be more dangerous and demoralizing than the fighting, military officials developed the idea of warming tents where combat troops could escape the bone-chilling temperatures. Warming tents were heated shelters behind the lines where men could go for a short time to thaw their frozen fingers and toes, write a letter, or sleep. Some of the shelters were also equipped with hot water so that soldiers could shower and get clean clothes.

Men welcomed the setup, but the shelters gave only brief pleasure. "There were so many of us and so few tents that it became impossible to stay in the tents long enough to even approach getting warm. It was always time to leave and go back on the line so someone else could use the tents,"[101] observes Fred Davidson.

On Reserve

Reserve—a few weeks of service behind the lines to rest and unwind—was more coveted than warming tents. Reserve was instituted to ensure that a small number of men did not suffer the brunt of the heavy fighting while other units sat idly by, their guns and energy untapped.

Reserve meant that a unit moved to a camp or base equipped with hot showers, clean clothes, comfortable bunks, and hot food. Such quarters were not particularly luxurious, but they were far enough from the fighting that men could be free of the fear of being attacked as they slept. Tony Herbert explains, "Reserve. It's a powerful word in a combat zone. . . . It's time to catch up, and to get your bearings. And a time to find out how the war is going for the rest of the division, and for the rest of the army, since a man in combat doesn't have much opportunity to look around him."[102]

For soldiers who had not bathed for weeks, showers were one of the high points of reserve. It took time to remove weeks of grime, but hot water and large bars of yellow soap helped. James Brady describes his feelings:

> I was naked for the first time in forty-six days. . . . The water was very hot and we stood under it, steam rising, men shouting and laughing and playing grabass, faces very brown under the long matted hair, bodies fish-belly white. . . . It was funny how few marines had really good builds. Hollywood wouldn't have cast many of us in a [John] Duke Wayne war movie.[103]

Reserve meant cleaning up, but it also meant periods of training, drilling, and listening to lectures designed to improve performance and morale. Relaxation time was provided, however, and movies were a common form of entertainment. Less common but more enjoyable were United Service Organizations (USO) tour-

ing shows that featured stars such as Bob Hope and Debbie Reynolds. A makeshift stage was usually hastily constructed for the performers, and the audience clustered at their feet, applauding, whistling, and enjoying the music, comic acts, and attractive young women who were always included. Brady remembers, "I was a New Yorker and I'd seen plenty of shows, but I'd never enjoyed theatre more than I did right there sitting cross-legged on the ground in the snow."[104]

Rest and Recuperation

In 1951 the U.S. military instituted a formal rest and recuperation (R&R) program for the troops. The decision was based on World War II studies showing that casualties increased when soldiers engaged in combat more than 180 days without relief.

Those who qualified for R&R were flown to Japan on air force transport planes for five days of "temporary duty" in one of several cities including Tokyo, Osaka, and Kokura. There they received clean uniforms, money, food, and a room on a base or in a hotel. Martin Russ, housed in the Kyoto Hotel, recalls, "A uniformed doorman opened the door. A bellboy took my small bag. . . . The lobby was more luxurious than that of the Statler in Buffalo [New York]."[105]

The trips were highly popular with soldiers, many of whom used the time to drink and strike up relationships with girls (thus earning R&R its nickname, Rejoice

American actress Marilyn Monroe poses with U.S. soldiers in Korea. Monroe and other celebrities came to Korea to entertain the troops.

and Regret). Russ remembers, "I went out and found a restaurant. . . . There were a group of young dolls seated at the next table. One was particularly attractive. We smiled and I beckoned, it was as simple as that. She spoke English surprisingly well. Her name, she said, was Judy."[106]

Other men such as veteran Bob Dean were more careful and conservative:

> There were bars, bars, bars, dancing pavilions, and gambling establishments. I tried the bars the first evening, then found the USO, where they offered choices of exclusive resorts less than a day away (by train) where one really could relax and, pos-

sibly, recuperate. So I chose one of these, the Aso Kanko Hotel, figured out how to catch a train, and went there for about 4 days.[107]

About eight hundred thousand U.S. troops took advantage of the R&R program, which ran between January 1951 and June 1953.

The "Big R"

As the war continued—and peace talks showed no signs of reaching agreement—

military leaders inaugurated a rotation program whereby men could return to the United States after a significant period of time served in Korea. Beginning in the fall of 1951, between fifteen and twenty thousand soldiers rotated home each month.

The "Big R," as it was nicknamed by the men, was based on a point system. A soldier had to earn thirty-six points to become eligible, and service anywhere in Korea earned a man two points a month. Service within the sound of enemy guns brought three points a month. Action on the front line of a major battlefield was worth four points per month. As a result, combat troops commonly served nine to twelve months, while support forces in the rear served about eighteen.

Those soldiers who qualified to leave saw rotation as a wonderful innovation— a chance to go home. Those who remained in the war, however, noticed that it had a negative effect on a unit's fighting spirit. Greater numbers of inexperienced men were constantly being introduced into units. Those men who knew they were going home sometimes put others in danger by their erratic behavior: Some became distracted and sloppy at their work. Some grew reckless, others superstitious or terribly cautious, fearful that they would be killed just as they were about to return home. Martin Russ comments, "Some short-timers have been known to literally hide in caves until it comes time for them to be taken to the rear."[108]

"No Justice!"

Men who were nearing the time they could return to the United States were sometimes reassigned to a position in the rear where they would not endanger themselves or others. Their fighting comrades who remained on the front lines were generally happy for them, believing they had earned the break.

Frontline attitudes toward those who served full-time in the rear were not as generous, however. Believed to be holding undemanding jobs that allowed plenty of time for fun, "office pogues" provoked nothing but anger and derision, as a letter from Norman Allen to his mother indicates: "To hear some son-of-a-bitch stationed in Pusan—where he is so safe he doesn't even carry a gun, has hot showers every day, sleeps in a steam heated room between sheets . . .—gets to go [on R&R] to Japan! My God! No justice! I'm beginning to hate those rear-echelon bastards as much, or more, than the Chinese!"[109]

Appreciated or scorned, behind-the-lines troops made the war machine tick in Korea. Their support of the entire military made them a vital, but often overlooked, element of the conflict.

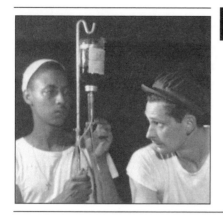

Chapter 5

24/7 Support

As many men and women served as cooks, helicopter pilots, clerks, and other support personnel as served in combat during the Korean War. Some of these enjoyed an easy existence, just as men on the front lines suspected. Others, however, worked around the clock, seven days a week, and sometimes sacrificed their lives in the course of their duties. No matter what their daily agenda, all were as committed to doing their part to win the war as any man on the MLR. "There was no glamour. I drew charts and flipped them at briefings," says Jim Byers, a statistical draftsman who gave air force pilots the intelligence information they needed to fly their missions. "I wasn't in the fighting. But passing information was, probably, the next most important thing in Korea."[110]

Support from the Air

Some of the most vital support troops were those who carried out air operations in the war. These operations were divided into several main categories that included transporting cargo and the wounded, engaging North Korean and Chinese Communist air forces, and bombing North Korea's military and industrial targets including bridges and hydroelectric plants. Thousands of air force personnel served in these operations. Over one thousand were killed in action during the war. Due to their work, however, many lives were saved and the enemy was significantly weakened.

Korea marked the first time that jet planes were used extensively in war, and jet fighter pilots were some of the most daring members of the military. Jet pilots were usually older than ordinary soldiers on the ground, and most had experience flying conventional airplanes during World War II. They were confident, self-motivated, and relatively defiant of rules—qualities that made them excellent at what they did. "We went up as a group as often as we could manage it. . . . We kept the MiGs [Soviet-made fighter jets] occupied in the northern part of Korea, away from our ground troops,"[111] states Colonel Robert Baldwin of the Fifty-first Fighter-Interceptor Group.

Many missions took place in the skies over North Korea. The airspace immediately south of the Yalu River—dubbed MiG Alley—was particularly popular with American fighters, who knew that many MiG bases were just across the river in China. Forbidden to cross the river to strafe or bomb them, pilots waited for planes to fly into Korean airspace and then attacked. Baldwin explains: "One way and another we gave the Chinese and North Koreans a hell of a bad time. The quality of their pilots began to fall off early on. . . . We lost people, no denying it. But by the time we were well settled in, we were killing ten MiGs for every Sabre lost. And by the end of the war, the kill ratio was sixteen to one."[112]

Troops parachute to earth with supplies and equipment during an air operation.

Bomber pilots also played important roles in Korea. From the first days of the war until just hours before a cease-fire was announced in 1993, they bombed supply trains, ammunition depots, runways, and other strategic enemy targets. Their assignments were usually highly dangerous as well, as pilot Bob Ennis recalls: "We lost planes all the time. Guys would get shot down, and some would make it back after bailing out, and others we'd never hear from again. They'd just never come back. In cases like that the aircraft probably ran into the ground, or hit the side of a mountain."[113]

Ennis flew nightly bombing raids in a two-engine B-26 Invader without benefit of night-vision technology, but he did not see himself as a daredevil: "I was never a tiger. I never took unnecessary chances. There's a saying, 'There are no old, bold pilots.' I would take any risk necessary to get the job done, but I tried not to be reckless. The odds of getting shot down or knocked down were bad enough already."[114]

A helicopter takes off after bringing U.S. troops to the war's front line. Helicopter pilots took great risks to carry out their missions.

Helicopter pilots were another category of expert flying men. Helicopters were first used during the Korean War to insert and remove troops from battles and to carry the wounded to mobile hospitals. Pilots had to be extremely skillful, and regularly risked their lives when they landed in "hot" zones in the heart of the fight. Bullets regularly hit their aircraft, and sometimes men were hit as well. "I wasn't a hero. I was scared. . . . It was unbelievable what we did out there. It was the beginning of helicopter warfare,"[115] states pilot Edward Barker.

When not flying, pilots and their crews lived on rough bases behind the front lines. They slept on cots in tents or corrugated metal huts, coped with mud and outdoor plumbing, and grabbed hot meals when they could. Their focus, however, was always on their missions. Everything else was secondary. "It was a case of getting up in the morning before daybreak, flying missions, coming back, sleeping when you could, and flying missions,"[116] Barker remembers.

Medics and MASH Units

Like pilots, army medics and navy corpsmen regularly put their lives in danger to aid the fighting men. Required on the front lines to bandage wounds, stanch bleeding, and provide other necessary first aid to the injured, these paramedics faced the same heat, cold, and rough conditions that combat troops endured. Their focus on helping others in battle, however, often made them vulnerable to enemy bullets. In the early weeks of the war, many who were inexperienced were killed, as Lacy Barnett remembers: "Instead of crawling to the men [who were wounded], the excited aidman would jump up and attempt to run to the next wounded man. It was then that he, too, would be hit by rifle fire or a shell burst. . . . It was tragic situation which occurred with depressing frequency."[117]

While medics could give only the most basic care to wounded men, doctors, nurses, and technicians who served in Mobile Army Surgical Hospital (MASH) units provided much broader medical services. They regularly removed shrapnel, sewed up wounds, treated illness, and evaluated those who were mentally or emotionally unstable. MASH units, designed to be the first line of care off the battlefield, were located throughout the country, usually near the battle lines. For instance, in the weeks after the Inchon invasion, the Forty-third MASH advanced up the Korean peninsula with the army, even at one time setting up camp in Pyongyang.

MASH doctors, nurses, and staff worked and lived in the most basic surroundings, as portrayed in the film *MASH* and the hit television series based on that film. They slept in tents with dirt floors, ate in mess halls, and stored their few possessions in crates or footlockers. They successfully performed operations and cared for patients in makeshift surgeries where sterile conditions were difficult to maintain. They

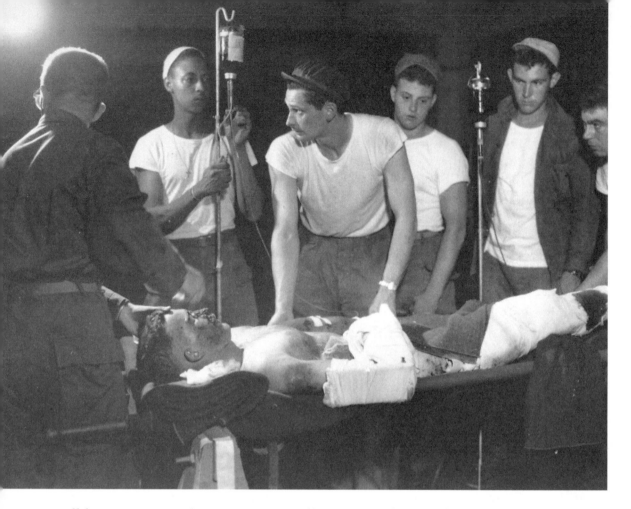

MASH doctors and nurses examine an injured soldier at a makeshift hospital in North Korea.

all became experts in emergency medicine of all kinds. Because the emphasis was on saving as many lives as possible, however, everyone concentrated on the most basic medical practices rather than sophisticated techniques. Captain H. Richard Hornberger, a former MASH surgeon, says, "We [were] not concerned with the ultimate reconstruction of the patient. We [were] concerned only with getting the kid out of here alive enough for someone else to reconstruct him."[118]

Several innovations helped doctors successfully practice better medicine during the war. Plastic bags to hold intra-venous solutions, including blood, made transportation and storage of these vital fluids easier and more readily available. Improvements in vascular surgery reduced the need for amputations. The decision to treat battle fatigue (stress disorder resulting from combat) with bed rest and hot food just behind the lines quickened men's ability to recover and return to duty. In World War II, such cases had been evacuated to the rear for extended periods of time. This practice had increased men's convictions that they were mentally ill and slowed the healing process.

Because they were constantly fighting to save lives, many doctors and nurses in MASH units, facing the sacrifice of human life that was a part of war, firsthand, felt futility and bitterness. In some units, this disillusionment led to sloppiness, poorly maintained equipment and supplies, and substandard cleanliness. In some instances, doctors and nurses also turned to alcohol as an escape from their feelings.

Other, more wholesome diversions were available, however, especially beginning in 1952 when the war became more static and units could remain in one locale for an extended period of time. Then, baseball diamonds, volleyball courts, and horseshoe pits were built. Movies and USO shows were available. And, as with other military forces, R&R to Japan was a regularly enjoyed break from routine.

Women in the War

MASH units were among the few places where military women served in Korea. The sixty thousand servicewomen in the war were not otherwise allowed on or near the front lines, and so they occupied support positions in Japan or, more rarely, in Pusan and Seoul. They worked as stenographers and interpreters, and in communications, intelligence, supply, and food service units. Some also became censors, parachute riggers, draftspersons, and weather personnel.

A large number were in medical service. Navy nurses worked aboard hospital ships in waters surrounding Korea. Air force nurses flew in and out of Korea on medical transport planes. Many American military nurses also staffed hospitals in Japan, where thousands of war casualties were transported.

The first MASH nurses arrived in Korea on July 5, 1950, four days after the arrival of Task Force Smith. They numbered fifty-seven and came to Pusan from Japan. After setting up the hospital and taking care of the first casualties, twelve moved north to Taejon, where hard fighting would soon take place.

By August, less than a month after the onset of hostilities, more than one hundred army nurses were on duty in South Korea in support of UN troops. The conditions they faced were much the same as those that fighting men endured at this time. Most wore fatigues (field uniforms), steel helmets, and combat boots rather than traditional uniforms. They ate out of aluminum mess kits, lived in tents or bombed-out buildings, washed in their helmets, and slept in sleeping bags. "We worked eight hours on and eight hours off for about a month before changing to 12 hours on and 12 hours off,"[119] remembers Julia Baxter, who also recalled times when more than one thousand wounded men were waiting for care in the yard outside the hospital.

Despite such hardships, these women remained focused on the war, and the men they were trying to help were always their first priority. One nurse from Emporia, Kansas, went home in August 1950, pleading for blood donations. She explained, "There has been a mass slaughter and massacre over here. You must realize how fighting mad it makes us when someone says we are not actually in a state of war. Technically, maybe this isn't a formal war, but I wish some of the men in Washington could see Korean conditions."[120]

In the Background

Conditions in Korea would have been worse were it not for other support personnel ranging from mechanics to military police (MPs). Office staff handled mail, paychecks, and leave assignments. Chaplains listened to confessions, led worship services, and comforted the grief-stricken. Supply clerks kept levels of ammunition available; made sure that plenty of C rations and food were on hand; and ordered new uniforms, boots, tents, and blankets. Drivers carried food and supplies to men at the front over dangerous roads exposed to enemy fire.

Some of the first support personnel in the war were members of the U.S. Army Corps of Engineers and the Naval Mobile Construction Battalions (NMCB), commonly known as Seabees. The latter were construction battalions that followed the marines into combat zones, building roads, living facilities, bridges, airstrips, and other necessary structures.

Bob Markey and his colleague, Terry Carroll, were both Seabee mechanics stationed near Seoul in the early months of the war. There, as part of the motor pool, they were directed to create a parts warehouse that could be used to keep war vehicles running. Markey described their work:

Each morning Terry and I would walk to the parts warehouse, carbines [rifles] slung over our shoulders, hang the weapons on a nearby wall, and begin to sort thousands of parts we had begged, borrowed and traded for at bases all over Korea. We soon became the place to find just about anything and were doing a fine business. We would trade a dozen spark plugs for a carburetor or a Jeep spring for a part for a dozer. We obtained cross-reference parts books and could find a General Motors truck part that was the same as a Ford part in a matter of minutes. It was fun work.[121]

The Seabees were builders, but their motto, "We build, we fight," meant that they also had to be prepared to defend themselves if the need arose. Markey's experience bore out this motto. He and several other Seabees were en route to relieve a work party in the hills one night when a large group of North Korean soldiers intercepted them. Outnumbered, the Americans drew their weapons and were ready to fight to the death when the North Koreans drove around them and disappeared down the road. Markey noted

Contrasting Expectations

While recovering from an ankle injury in a hospital unit, Captain Norman Allen had time to rest and examine the expectations of frontline soldiers compared with those of men in the rear. In a letter to his mother, included in Donald Knox's *The Korean War: Pusan to Chosin*, he tries to explain why such expectations were different.

On the front lines the very little things, extra water, some gum, a few cigars, and maybe an occasional hot meal and the men are insanely happy. Troops in the rear with cots, roofs over their heads, hot-water showers, bitch and raise hell cause they don't get enough beer. Actually, it's not so unreasonable, just the troops at the various echelons live at such varied standards. What it takes to please the frontline soldier with the lowest standard, wouldn't even faze a rear-line soldier. A little thing like a night without fear is looked upon as a golden apple and about as rare."

Luxuries like these cans of beer were not always evenly distributed among U.S. troops.

later, "We had looked into the face of death and stared it down. . . . We were damn lucky, but we had held our ground in the tradition of all the Seabees who had gone before us. And we were proud of ourselves."[122]

Garments and Graves

Less in evidence than the Seabees, laundry and bath platoons were nevertheless much appreciated by frontline troops.

Equipped with pumps, boilers, washing machines, and portable showers, these men traveled just behind the lines and offered the opportunity to bathe, get rid of fleas or lice, and change into clean clothes. Quartermaster Lieutenant Kenneth O. Schellberg explained that soldiers did not carry changes of clothing in their duffel bags, and thus relied on these mobile clothing exchanges for everything from socks to uniforms:

A soldier plays "Taps" over rows of graves. Digging plots for fallen soldiers became so common that an entire graves detail was maintained throughout the war.

There were many advantages to the clothing exchange system. It cut down the weight the soldier had to carry; it also eliminated duffel bags and the thirty-man detail in each regiment to guard and handle them. This increased our mobility. The cleaner clothing improved the hygiene of the troops. . . . The shower and clothing exchange was a great morale builder for the men.[123]

While laundry personnel took care of the living, the men of graves registration were assigned the task of tending to the dead. They not only identified those who were killed, they were responsible for mailing personal effects to families and seeing that the bodies were properly buried until they could be shipped home.

Graves registration staff was daily surrounded by the graphic evidence of the carnage of war. Although they learned to face their responsibilities without flinching, Sergeant Bill Chambers notes that he was at first unprepared for the gruesomeness of the assignment. "They wanted to break us in, get us used to seeing these things. So they took us to the army mortuary. . . . Let me tell you, it didn't help.

You thought it helped, until you saw what bodies looked like on the battlefield."[124]

The men of graves registration were not commonly in the heart of battles; litter bearers in combat units usually gathered up their own dead and carried them behind the lines. Nevertheless, some aspects of the job were dangerous and frightening, as Chambers explains: "Sometimes we found men with grenades still in their hands, with the pin pulled. . . . We'd have to slide a pin back in that thing and pry the fingers off of it. It used to scare us a little, because one mistake and there'd be two dead bodies there instead of one."[125]

Safe and Secure

Support personnel who worked in office settings on bases or in reserve camps saw little of the ugliness that medics, doctors, and graves registration units experienced. Their living conditions were not luxurious, but they were usually clean and warm, their food was palatable, and the danger they faced was low level.

Their days followed established routines. Sergeant Leonard Korgie recalls, "I got out of the sack around 6:30 AM, having slept through the night, put my boots on, and woke the other three men in the tent—a clerk/typist and two field men." After getting dressed, the men breakfasted in the mess tent, then had time to relax, smoke, and chat about the day's events for a time. Korgie remarks, "I hated wearing my helmet; it mussed up my carefully combed hair. I regularly pol-

ished my boots and washed my clothes. I was well fed and rested; ten miles behind the MLR I felt tough as hell."[126]

Korgie was not the only man to enjoy a comfortable life behind the lines. For a time, Luther Weaver began his day with a battalion staff meeting, and then he and his driver would proceed to a nearby supply depot to gather items that would later be taken to the front lines—sandbags, logs for building bunkers, clean socks, boots, underwear, and the like. By afternoon Weaver's duties were complete, and he would take a shotgun that he had found in the supply trailer and go pheasant hunting in the nearby fields. One of his most memorable experiences was shooting two pheasant in front of an audience of men from his company: "After much handshaking with many of the men I knew by name, I gave Joe Wlox, the mess sergeant, the birds I had with me and told him to treat Love Company to a pheasant dinner."[127]

Those who lived in safety behind the lines were usually referred to derogatorily as "REMFs" ("Rear-Echelon Mother F——s") by the fighting men. Rear-echelon workers were seen as doing little but "pushing paper" and enforcing senseless rules. They were believed to have no notion of what life on the front lines was like. This stereotype was reinforced by men like an unnamed staff officer who visited an infantry unit involved in heavy fighting in 1951. Covered in smoke and grime like the rest of his unit, Sergeant Gilbert Isham remembers: "All at once coming up the hill is a spic and span picture soldier. His fatigues were pressed to a knife crease. He had a powder blue scarf around his neck. His helmet had been freshly painted. His boots were spit shined."[128]

Despite the negative stereotyping, soldiers who served in the rear usually worked hard, and many were frustrated that they did not get to fight. Private Webster Manuel, a switchboard operator in Headquarters Company, states:

> I was in the commo (communications) section, and at Chipyong-ni assigned as a switchboard operator, which I hated like hell because I had reen-

listed and volunteered for Korea to see some action. I particularly disliked it whenever the regimental XO (executive officer), Lieutenant Colonel Metzer, would ring the switchboard and greet the operator, "Hello, girls!"—this would chap my ass to no end.[129]

At least one soldier refused to serve in such a support position. Anthony Herbert was told to report to a communications unit near Pusan when he arrived in Korea in 1951. His reaction was disbelief: "I hadn't come to Korea to repair radios, and I wasn't about to sit out the war in Pusan. There were plenty of guys around

The "Niceties" of Life

Battery executive officer Bob Dean was responsible for the training and performance of the howitzer (artillery) crews and Fire Direction Center (FDC) personnel who plotted targets and translated coordinates into commands for the gunners. Stationed behind the lines, Dean was given his own private bunker and a Korean houseboy who cleaned his quarters and washed his clothes. As Dean relates, he also had access to many inexpensive "niceties" that frontline soldiers did not see in the war.

> I bought a radio from someone going home, for $10. It had been converted to be operable with GI radio batteries and provided the popular songs of the day in our FDC, thanks to the Armed Forces Radio Network. When I left I sold it to my replacement. For $10.
>
> I bought several other things, one at a time, from the Battery PX [Post Exchange]. It was

a small "store," managed by the Administrative Warrant Officer, and open about an hour each day. As the spring wore on, I bought a pair of Ray-Ban sunglasses (for $6; worth $12), a Kodak 35mm. camera ($50), and a Parker ballpoint pen for $6. Almost bought a Smith Corona portable typewriter but, after trying it out on a few letters home, decided against it.

The PX also sold various "sundries," like toothpaste and razor blades, stationery and such. One week, a big supply of aftershave came in—and was gone within minutes. We later found out why: our very, very, capable Chief of Firing Battery had purchased and consumed it all. After such totally uncharacteristic behavior, he was found unconscious in his bunk. He woke up [demoted to] a corporal and began his climb back to the rank he (most of the time) richly deserved.

who would be happy with those orders."[130] Herbert soon went AWOL (absent without leave) to another unit. There he managed to get to the fighting, where he remained and became the most decorated American soldier in military history.

Anthony Herbert was in the minority in his willingness to break the rules to get into combat. By late 1952 most men were willing, but not eager, to fight. They had begun to wonder why they were risking their lives in a war they were not allowed to win. They were often put on the defensive by friends and family members, too, who did not understand the logic of limited warfare. One veteran recalls:

> My family and friends were concerned about Korea, but more important, they were confused about it. They couldn't understand the losing, the winning, the losing, the winning. . . . I kept my mouth shut. They would have to learn about limited conventional warfare themselves. They would have to get the drift without my help. How could I explain it? I didn't understand it, myself.[131]

Chapter 6

Sick and Tired

Most American soldiers had had little notion of what war involved when they first arrived in Korea. They knew that they would be "killing Commies," and the thought was exciting to some. But many had never been in combat before and had never killed any man, enemy or not. They soon discovered that the whole thing was more depressing, exhausting, and desensitizing than they had imagined. Corporal Mario Sorrentino relates his change of viewpoint: "I remembered how anxious I was to get to Korea. I was eighteen and couldn't wait to see combat. That lasted until the first firefight. Afterward it was, Please, God, don't let me get hurt."[132]

Days filled with violence and death, hatred of the enemy, intolerance, and other forms of negative behavior took their toll. So much ugliness, uncertainty, and loss left many with scars that would never completely heal. As army medic Lloyd Kreider explains, "People think

they have problems, but most people don't know what real suffering is. People like that aren't going to understand what I went through. They say, 'Oh, yeah, I know, I read about that.' Well, you can read about it all you want, but you're not going to understand how it was."[133]

Broken by War

Even the toughest men were tortured by loneliness, uncertainty, and fear in the war. Despite such feelings, most obeyed orders and did their part to win. The effort sometimes had a permanent effect on their energy and outlook, however, as the case of one Sergeant Fitzgerald illustrates. Fitzgerald was a promising athlete who hoped to attend college on an athletic scholarship. He abandoned his dream after months on the front lines, however, settling instead for something easier to achieve. "I thought I'd go up to the Ford Motor Company and maybe get me a job," he told a friend. "They got a plant up near Flint [Michigan] and they say they need plant police around there, you know, security and so on."[134]

Some men did not hold up as well as Fitzgerald. They gave in to their fear or lack of commitment and tried to get out of the fighting. Some went AWOL, believing that even if they were caught, time in prison was better than time at the front.

Some tried to fake illness or injury. A few even went a step further. Private Floyd Akins remembers a new addition to their regiment who shot himself in the foot shortly after his arrival: "I think he did it

A U.S. soldier writes a letter in the doorway of his bunker. Receiving and sending mail helped many soldiers combat the loneliness they felt throughout the war.

"Murder in My Heart"

As fighting continued, some soldiers became angry, not just at the enemy, but at U.S. leaders who seemed unable to bring the war to an end. One of those angry men was Seymour "Hoppy" Harris, a gunner with Company H, Twenty-third Infantry Regiment in 1951. What follows is an excerpt of a letter he wrote to a friend. The complete article appears on the Korean War Project website.

> During the Punchbowl operations, casualties were high and action heavy, yet the radio in the States was saying, "Limited patrol action in Korea last night, casualties very light." On this day as we waited for what seemed like an eternity for help to arrive and the choppers to take out the nearly dead, the sun seemed about to cook us alive. The wounded were moaning, praying, and calling out for "Mother." I had time to

do a little soul searching, and whenever I did that, I did crazy things. This time I was sitting there with murder in my heart for the politicians who had blundered me into this mess, when a sniper bullet plowed into the ground about three feet from me.

> I stood slowly up to my full height, and looking up the hill where the round had come from, commenced to yell at the top of my voice. . . .

> Crack! Zing! He drops one at my feet.

> "You missed again, you stupid rat eating SOB."

> I must have gone clear out of it because next thing I know I find myself walking along up the trail that leads to our bunkers with a guy on each arm.

on purpose. That first day he said he wouldn't be in Korea long."[135]

Some men fought for a time, then became "shook"—developed battle fatigue characterized by nervousness, anxiety, and fear. A few had hallucinations. Some exhibited bizarre behaviors. James Brady suggests the cause: "It was 76s [shells] coming in flat and fast or mortars dropping on you or fear of mines or maybe too many . . . night ambushes or a wind that never stopped blowing. Those were things that made you 'shook,' everyone agreed."[136] An extreme case involved a once-reliable soldier who suddenly refused to get out of his sleeping bag. He continued to carry out his daily duties by cutting out the bottom of the bag so he

could walk around, but insisted on keeping the bag over his head for protection.

Only the thought of loved ones at home got some men through the hard times, and when that support failed, many were devastated. One young artillery gunner became depressed after receiving a "Dear John" letter from his fiancée. He responded by writing back: "There are 500,000 N. Koreans and Chinese on the other side of that hill bound and determined to make sure I don't have a future."[137] Two days later, he charged a Chinese machine-gun position and was instantly killed.

Hundreds of Bodies

In addition to coping with fear and uncertainty, all who took part in the fighting had to come to grips with death and loss. Dead bodies were regularly a part of the landscape, whether they were former friends or enemies. Beverly Scott describes a scene on Heartbreak Ridge: "There were bodies strewn all over the place. Hundreds of bodies frozen in the snow. We could see the arms and legs sticking up. Nobody could get their dead out of there."[138]

Most men tried to remain sensitive to death, but the sight of bodies soon became routine. "I saw a six-by truck full of frozen bodies waiting to move out," says Private John Bishop, describing an incident near the Chosin Reservoir. "It looked like a load of meat going to market. I saw a Marine strapped over the barrel of a howitzer. He was covered by a poncho, all but his stiff legs. It reminded me of a deer carcass tied to the top of a car."[139]

Despite the hardening process, men seldom got used to the suffering of the wounded. Private John Kamperschroer recalls, "One of the most disturbing things I saw was a fellow brought in who had lost both legs to a mortar round which dropped into his foxhole. He and his buddy were laying head to toe to each other. Of course, the round had killed his buddy. I remember the poor soul asking over and over how his buddy was. No one had the heart to tell him."[140]

Many times a fellow soldier lay mangled and bleeding and nothing could be done for him until it was too late. Norman Allen remembers being pinned down by the enemy while he and his men had to listen as a wounded man in their unit endured a painful death: "I lay there helpless, numb, sick clear through. . . . The man died a little boy, wanting his mother, crying for her, asking for his God. That night has left a long, deep scar."[141]

The loss of a close friend in battle was traumatic for everyone. Those who experienced such a loss reacted in various ways. Some took it quietly, grieving deeply but accepting the loss as one of the things that made war a nightmare. Some became angry and vengeful. Some denied their losses, at least for a time. Lieutenant Charles Payne recounts an incident involving a young man who lost his buddy: "He wouldn't, or couldn't, put him down, just kept adding bandages to his wounds. I told him we needed his rifle, his buddy was dead, and he had to get into the fight. This went on for some time. Finally, I made him join us. He cursed me badly and said he'd settle with me later. He would not believe his friend was dead."[142]

Death caused by friendly fire—a mistaken attack on men by their own planes or artillery—was perhaps even harder to accept. Friendly fire incidents, made worse by the confusion of the war during its first months, produced many casualties in Korea.

Charles Payne was able to comment firsthand on this also. His unit had been fighting against almost impossible odds on August 6, 1950, and just when conditions seemed hopeless, an American tank appeared around the curve of the road near an old gristmill where they had taken cover. Rejoicing that he and his men were saved, Payne's joy quickly changed to horror when the tank opened fired on them, wounding him and killing several others: "A sergeant, I believe his name was Cartwright, had been scrapping great all day, inspiring each of us with his guts. That damned tank fired a round. It crashed into the mill and hit Cartwright in the waist. The explosion was the last thing in the mill I remember."[143]

Leadership Trouble

In the midst of trying to stay alive, American soldiers struggled to understand the conflict that had arisen between President Truman and General Douglas MacArthur over the way the war should be fought. The disagreement was disquieting, especially when men were putting their lives on the line to carry out plans that they hoped were brilliantly laid and expertly managed.

Many men felt extremely loyal to MacArthur. He was one of them, and his experience and his victories were legendary. Lacy Barnett was one of many who put his doubts aside when he spoke of the general: "MacArthur told everyone there would be one more push and that we would all be home for Christmas. In our bull sessions we concluded that Russia and China would not . . . permit South Korea to gain control over the north. The Communists were not that

dumb. However, we all felt maybe General MacArthur knew something we did not know and, in fact, we would be home for Christmas."[144]

Like MacArthur, soldiers also liked the idea of scoring a decisive victory over the enemy. They knew that America had won all its wars and felt it ought to win this one as well. They questioned whether limits should be placed on where they could fight and what weapons they would use.

Despite their loyalty to the general, however, all realized that as military men, they were bound by honor to obey President Truman. He was their commander in chief, as Private Herbert Luster explains:

> People asked my opinion about Truman firing MacArthur. I had to find an opinion, even though I'd only been a private and knew little about the political infighting going on while I was fighting the war. I recalled I had taken an oath to serve the United States and to obey the orders of my commander [Truman]. Since Mac had once taken the same pledge, I was forced to agree with the president, even though I was all for going right to Moscow to bring the war to an end once and for all.[145]

Discrimination and Prejudice

Confusion and a host of other negative emotions often brought out the worst in American soldiers. One of the most objec-

A Terrible Thing

Racist attitudes were so widespread among Americans in 1950 that racism was taken for granted in the Korean War. Harry Summers of Company L witnessed its effect on black soldiers' self-image one memorable night in 1950. His story is included in Rudy Tomedi's book *No Bugles, No Drums*.

I was in a three-man foxhole with one other guy, and they dropped this new replacement off at our foxhole. The other guy I was in the foxhole with was under a poncho, making coffee. It was bitterly cold. And pitch dark. He got the coffee made, and he gave me a drink, and he took a drink, and then he offered some to this new replacement, who we literally couldn't see, it was that dark.

And the guy said, "No, I don't want any."

"What the hell are you talking about, you don't want any? You got to be freezing to death, Here, take a drink of coffee."

"No," the guy said. . . . "You can't tell it now, but I'm black. And tomorrow morning when you find out I was drinking out of the same cup you were using, you ain't gonna be too happy."

". . . . You silly son of a bitch," we told him, "here, take the goddamn coffee."

That was our first black replacement. And it really struck me, then, what a terrible, terrible thing we'd done to ourselves, and to our society. That a man would come to us with an attitude like that.

Most African American soldiers experienced some degree of racism while stationed in Korea.

tionable attitudes to arise was racism, not only toward North and South Koreans but toward black American soldiers as well.

Racial discrimination was common in the United States in the 1950s, and the civil rights movement had not yet drawn widespread support. President Truman had ordered the integration of the military in 1948, but some units were still segregated into all-black or all-Caucasian membership, and black soldiers were often given menial positions or assignments that put them in greater danger than whites. They were also poorly trained and supplied, which sometimes adversely affected their performance in the field.

Such poor performance was commonly used as proof that African American troops were inferior fighters. When the all-black Twenty-fourth Infantry Regiment made a panicky retreat in the Battle of Taejon in July 1950, they became the object of jokes, despite the fact that other all-white units also retreated in disarray at the beginning of the war. Even a song, "Bugout Boogie," was written to ridicule them. The lyrics read, "When the Commie mortars start to chug, The ol' Deuce Four begin to bug, . . . When you hear the pitter-patter of little feet, It's the ol' Deuce Four in full retreat."[146]

Black soldiers naturally resented such slurs but tolerated them because the consideration and opportunities they were given in the military were better than what they were used to at home. Much racist behavior stemmed from Caucasian superiors and so was overlooked for the sake of careers. Beverly Scott relates, "There were always the really outright racist sons of bitches. But you didn't deal with those people. You maintained a strictly professional relationship and had no interpersonal dealings at all with that kind of officer."[147]

At least one of their superiors, Matthew Ridgway, was more than willing to treat blacks as equals. In 1951, faced with a lack of fighting men, he directed that blacks be integrated into all fighting units throughout the war zone. The order did not erase intolerance and discrimination,

but it helped. Caucasians who had never had to rely on black fellow soldiers before soon learned that they were just as intelligent, reliable, and hard-fighting as whites. Eventually most men found the color of a man's skin irrelevant. Grant Hauskins remembers: "In the heat of battle, you don't have time to discriminate; you only have time to try to stay alive. That's what was going on in Korea. There were isolated cases there just as now. You can always find some isolated case where you're going to have a redneck who is going to voice his opinion."[148]

ROKs and North Koreans

The racial prejudice that Caucasian soldiers exhibited toward Koreans and Chinese—whom they dubbed "gooks" and "chinks"—stemmed partly from prejudice against Asians that existed in the United States and partly from a lasting hatred of the Japanese from World War II. Even South Korean soldiers, who were American allies, were unfairly perceived as sneaky, unreliable, and inferior. Blaine Friedlander, a teacher from Virginia, notes, "My memory is, the American soldier hated the Korean soldier. And the dislike was automatic, because some of the guys making those remarks had never come near a Korean outfit. They hated Koreans by reflex action."[149]

Friedlander's attitude was an exception to the typical American disdain of Koreans. A member of the Korean Military Advisory Group (KMAG), he worked to help train ROK soldiers. Although he recognized vast differences between their culture and that of the United States, he also came to appreciate their intelligence and their civility:

> Once I was able to communicate with them I realized they were not a bunch of faceless gooks, but people who cared very deeply about their country, who knew its history and who also knew a surprising amount about our country, much more than the average American knew about Korea. They were not an army of dumb peasants.[150]

It was perhaps more understandable that American soldiers grew to hate North Koreans and Chinese, who were the enemy and were known to commit atrocities against captured Americans. After Floyd Akins found that North Koreans had shot his company commander in the back of the head, he reacted strongly: "I told a lieutenant standing next to me I was now ready to fight the North Koreans to the death if that's what it took. . . . Since that day I don't think I've ever been the same."[151]

There was abundant evidence that North Koreans carried out atrocities

Jack Todd, chief of the War Crimes Division in Korea, points to pictures exhibiting the atrocities North Korean and Chinese soldiers committed on UN prisoners of war.

against American and South Korean soldiers despite the fact that the Geneva Conventions called for civilians and prisoners to be treated humanely during wartime. Captured American soldiers were often found dead with their hands bound by wire, shot in the back of the head, and dumped in a ditch. Some had been tortured. Some were captured and endured brutal treatment.

Lloyd Kreider was among the latter. An army medic, he arrived in Korea in July 1950 and was taken captive in August. After three months of beatings, forced marches, and starvation, he and a group of American prisoners were herded aboard

freight cars and taken into a tunnel. Kreider recalls, "They'd decided to kill us all in that tunnel, and they were hoping we'd suffocate from the smoke from the engine. Some of the boys did die, but . . . we weren't dying fast enough." Those who survived were taken off the train and shot. Kreider managed to escape by playing dead. His return to safety was little short of a miracle. "I'd been a prisoner for only three months, but I looked like a walking dead man,"[152] he remembers.

South Korean civilians lie dead after being attacked by Communist troops.

Kreider's case was not unique. In an incident in August 1950, forty-two American soldiers were executed by North Koreans on Hill 303 near Waegwan, South Korea. And in several instances in November 1950, men near the Chosin Reservoir were taken captive and forced to march for days on end with little food despite injuries and illness. Corporal Lawrence Donovan remembers, "Not one night passed but there were shots—executions of the prisoners too weak to go on. . . . We kept walking because . . . we understood that to fall out of the line of march was a sure way to get a bullet in the neck from the guards."[153]

American Inhumanity

Most American soldiers followed the rules of the Geneva Conventions, but there were some who committed inhumane acts out of fear, confusion, or sheer brutality. The former motivations were most common. For instance, one soldier recounts that one day as a group of what appeared to be Korean refugees approached his platoon, he saw a small girl walking toward him. She held a grenade with no pin in her hands. Assuming that she might throw it, the soldier shot her. "I put a bullet in between her eyes," he said. "She bothers me to this day."[154]

Others obeyed orders even though they knew they were morally wrong. For instance, Corporal Logan Parnell was directed to kill an old man found hiding under a bridge. He reluctantly shot the old man in the head. Later, he was tortured by feelings of guilt: "After I settled down. I couldn't sleep. Nearby two officers quietly spoke to each other. I heard one say, 'That Marine had to shoot the old man.' The other said, 'I don't think I could do that.' . . . On the road [next day] I tried to swagger. We passed hundreds of Korean civilians. They all seemed to look at me."[155]

One of the worst, and most controversial, incidents of American atrocity occurred at a bridge near the village of No Gun Ri in July 1950, just days after the start of the war. Families of South Korean victims later alleged that soldiers rounded up a group of villagers and then called air fire down on them while they huddled in tunnels and culverts under the bridge. Anyone who came into the open was shot at. An estimated four hundred men, women, and children were killed in the incident. Edward Daily, a soldier who claimed to have taken part in the shooting, described the scene: "Even above the noise of the gun, I could hear the frightful screams of women and children crying out with pain and fear. Their dying voices echoed out of the tunnels. There were at least a couple of hundred lying in there."[156]

Undoubtedly, an atrocity occurred at No Gun Ri, where innocent civilians were shot by American soldiers. There is no certainty, however, that a massacre was ordered by the military. The Korean peninsula was in chaos at the time. Tens of thousands of South Koreans were fleeing advancing

North Korean forces, and North Korean infiltrators had been discovered among them. Inexperienced American forces, as a result, were jittery and could have panicked and shot into the group.

Confusion also exists over how many civilians were hurt. Eyewitness accounts have not held up to scrutiny. For instance, Edward Daily proved unreliable when it was learned he was in fact eighty miles away from No Gun Ri on the day of the shooting. Another soldier who claimed to have taken part in the killing had been evacuated from Korea the day before the incident.

Amid unresolved doubts, the episode was finally closed on January 11, 2001, when President Bill Clinton issued the following statement:

> On behalf of the United States of America, I deeply regret that Korean civilians lost their lives at No Gun Ri in late July 1950. The intensive, year-long investigation into this incident has served as a painful reminder of the tragedies of war and the scars they leave behind on people and on nations.
>
> Although we have been unable to determine precisely the events that occurred at No Gun Ri, the U.S. and South Korean governments have concluded . . . that an unconfirmed number of innocent Korean refugees were killed or injured there. To those Koreans who lost loved ones at No Gun Ri, I offer my condolences. . . . I sincerely

hope that the memorial the United States will construct to these and all other innocent Korean civilians killed during the war will bring a measure of solace [comfort] and closure.[157]

Guilty Pleasure

With so much hate, sorrow, and other unexamined emotions churning inside, it was no wonder that when it came time for men to rotate out of the war and return home, happiness was sometimes shaded by remorse and guilt. All knew that they were leaving friends behind to continue the fight, and questioned their own duty to see the conflict through to the end. Many could not forget the memories of those who would never be going home. Lieutenant Edmund Krekorian writes, "An uncontrolled wave of grief and depression came over me. I could no longer repress the memories of the men I'd known who had been killed. I felt overwhelming guilt that I had survived."[158]

Despite their emotional turmoil, the final day in Korea finally arrived. Aboard the plane or ship that took them home, returnees looked forward to better days. Most were excited. Some anticipated a hero's welcome. Few understood that, in the months and years ahead, America would act as if the war had never been. As Sergeant Earl Croft remembered, "We returned to our homeland and were rebuffed by many for not winning our war as had all ancestors before us. . . . We became the men who fought the 'Forgotten War.'"[159]

Chapter 7

The Forgotten War

The year 1953 began with 768,000 UN troops facing over 1 million Communist fighters along battle lines that had remained virtually the same for two years. In the peace talks, an unwillingness to compromise on both sides stalled negotiations for months at a time. As one issue was settled, another arose. "The truce talks drag endlessly, seeming always nearer to peace, and yet not settling a thing—I don't know, it's a senseless war at best, and it's not really accomplishing a lot, except to kill off some more of our boys,"[160] Private Jack Train Jr. wrote home in June 1953.

The situation remained tense until July 10, when UN negotiators were finally able to hammer out a settlement for an armistice, a temporary suspension of hostilities. After the longest peace talks in history, on Monday, July 27, representatives from all sides signed copies of the truce. A cease-fire went into effect twelve hours later.

In Korea, soldiers had been notified that the cease-fire would begin at 10:00 P.M.

Artillery fire continued until shortly before the appointed hour. Then, when the moment arrived, both sides shot off flares, and the shooting stopped.

A few minutes later, some men took a chance and climbed up until they were dangerously silhouetted against the skyline. Others waited until morning to investigate. Marine corporal Robert Hall was one of the latter. He recalls, "At first we stood in the trenches. Then some climbed up to the forward edges, then to the tops of the bunkers, for a better look. It was unheard of—standing in the open in the daylight. . . . Then to look, and eventually walk through the land ahead of the trenches, a thing that would have meant sure death 24 hours before. That's when we began to realize that it was really over."[161]

"Moment of Sober Satisfaction"

Truman's "police action" ended three years, one month, and two days after it started. It had cost the president much in terms

U.S. soldiers celebrate the cease-fire in Korea. After the fighting went on for more than three years, negotiators finally reached an armistice in 1953.

of popularity. He had chosen not to run for office in 1952, and General Dwight D. Eisenhower had been elected the nation's thirty-fourth president.

The United States paid a high price for the war in many ways beyond its $67 billion cost. Fifty-four thousand Americans were dead, and over one hundred thousand were injured, almost as many as would be killed in fourteen years of fighting in Vietnam in the 1960s and 1970s. Over five thousand men were missing, neither side had gained significant ground, and neither could claim a definitive victory.

Nevertheless, America had been successful in its original purpose: South Korea had been saved from Communist aggression. Eisenhower, who had visited Korea in late 1952 to help end the war, told Americans it was a "moment of sober satisfaction."[162]

Most of the men who returned home after the war felt satisfaction as well. They knew they had done a patriotic and honorable thing by serving their country and fighting communism. They also realized that the war had offered them learning experiences that they might not have gotten elsewhere. They had grown up, forged new friendships, and gained a new perspective on life. "While I wouldn't want to go through the Korean War experience again, I'm glad that I had the chance," observes Angelo Miglietta:

As a white northerner, I got a much broader understanding of race relationships. . . . I appreciate now that

Families of U.S. troops greet a ship carrying soldiers to California from Korea.

most people will accept responsibility, even when it is thrust upon them without much chance for preparation. If people are asked to do difficult tasks, most people will accept the challenge and do the best they can. Most people have an inherent pride in doing a good job, even at great risk.[163]

The Silent Veterans

Men like Miglietta did not expect cheering crowds and ticker-tape parades upon their return, but they hoped to be received with a certain amount of gratitude and respect, just as other veterans had been granted respect after past wars. At first such recognition seemed attainable. Edmund Krekorian describes his arrival in Seattle with one of the first shiploads of returning veterans: "We felt honored, appreciated, and recognized for our efforts. There were hundreds of people on the pier. Flags, division crests, and pennants hung everywhere. A large sign read, 'Welcome Home, Defenders of Freedom.' Miss Seattle with a bouquet of flowers met the ship, and a band played the National Anthem."[164]

Later returnees, however, discovered that most Americans had become indifferent. The end of the war was not a glorious triumph to be celebrated. Its end seemed unimportant compared to other events that had made recent headlines—the death of Soviet premier Joseph Stalin, the Rosenberg spy trial, Senator Joseph McCarthy's claims that Communists had infiltrated the federal government, and

the blacklisting of actors and actresses suspected of Communist sympathies.

Some people had not realized what a terrible struggle the war had been. Some even mistakenly assumed that it had concluded long before. The return of Korean War veterans thus went largely unnoticed and uncelebrated. "We were the silent veterans of the forgotten war. It [our return] was like a rock thrown into a pond and there wasn't a ripple,"[165] explains combat photographer Frank Kerr.

Overlooked Warriors

Rather than become resentful, most veterans took the lack of attention in stride and quietly resumed the routines of working and raising their families. They were surprised by how little the war meant to most Americans, but they accepted the fact with a philosophical shrug. "We were just kind of forgotten, but it never bothered me," says John Dollar, a sergeant in the conflict. "Everyone was sick of war."[166]

A few veterans did not react so positively. They grew angry when they realized that their accomplishments and their sacrifice had been overlooked. "What really surprised me was how many of my relatives and friends couldn't believe Korea was a 'real war,' that I had actually been in combat," says Sergeant Leonard Korgie. "In fact, some of them were very puzzled by the ribbons I wore on my uniform."[167]

Some veterans found that they could not put their wartime experience behind them, especially if they had lost limbs or suffered some other serious injury that affected their health or prevented them from working. Others repeatedly recalled the disturbing sights and sounds of suffering and dying that they had witnessed in combat. They began experiencing nightmares. They turned to alcohol to try to forget. They fought with their wives and went through divorces.

In later years, many of these men would learn that their troubles had been given a medical name—post-traumatic stress disorder, a psychological condition common to some degree among individuals who have experienced or witnessed profoundly traumatic events. In the 1950s, that syndrome was unrecognized and went largely untreated. Most veterans had to cope with their symptoms—flashbacks, nightmares, irritability, anxiety, fatigue, forgetfulness, and social alienation—as best they could. "I tried to live a 'normal life,' even though I had flashbacks and nightmares of insane killings. . . . When the problems persisted, I went to the Veterans Administration for help. There I was told they could not help me,"[168] remembers Corporal Albert Glick, who survived fighting at the Chosin Reservoir.

Even some who did not experience traumatic episodes eventually came to feel bitter about the fact that life had gone on without them while they had been in the war. The U.S. economy had boomed in the early 1950s. Friends who had not gone to Korea had gotten good

Not Forgotten

In an editorial in the New Brunswick, New Jersey, *Sentinel*, posted on the paper's website, Carl J. Asszony, Middlesex County Veterans Services coordinator, points out that while the Korean War has been ignored by a majority of Americans, untold numbers remember it all too clearly.

To many people, the Korean War is still "the forgotten war." But to the 54,000 American families whose loved ones died in Korea, it is not forgotten. For the 100,000 Americans who returned home maimed or wounded, it is not forgotten. For those fighting men who suffered the hardship of the bitter winds and battle fatigue during combat in the mountains of Korea, it is not forgotten. For those who suffered the horrors of prisoner of war camps from which only half of the 7,000 prisoners returned home, it is not forgotten. For those who battled on Pork Chop Hill or Heartbreak Ridge, it is not forgotten. For the pilots who flew daily sorties to help stem the tide of the North Korean forces, it is not forgotten. For the families of the 8,200 missing in action, it is not forgotten. For the doctors, nurses and hundreds of support groups who served there, it is not forgotten. For those who saw the carnage and slaughter of millions of civilians on both sides, it is not forgotten. For the 1.5 million who served in the military during that period, it is not forgotten.

jobs, had been given promotions, and were well on their way to successful careers. Veterans had been left behind. "Eventually I got over my resentment about Korea," notes Vincent Walsh, a navy machinist. "About the way we were treated

Problems of the Past

Men who suffered from post-traumatic stress disorder upon their return from Korea were forced to cope with their problems without support or aid from the government. In *Korean Vignettes: Faces of War*, Albert Glick describes his ordeal and the steps he took to recover.

> I tried to go on with my life, was married in 1956, and started my family. But when the problems persisted, I went to the Veterans Administration for help. There I was told they could not help me. I was referred to San Diego County where I was committed to a state mental hospital. I was there for some eight months and did get some group therapy, but no effort was ever made to find the cause of my problems. I was never questioned about my service in Korea. Many years later, of course after the Viet Nam War and the return of those veterans, the experts came up with a name for the condition, i.e., Post Traumatic Stress Disorder. . . .
>
> Eventually, I worked through my problems on my own, and with my wife, became involved in our sons' Little League and other family pursuits. Over the years I was able to bury the problems of the past. After joining some Korean War Veterans' organizations in the late 80s and early 90s I realized I had really lost something, some part of me. . . . The feeling of frustration and anger is hard to imagine.

Many soldiers had trouble adjusting to civilian life following their tours in Korea.

after we got back home. It wasn't as bad as Vietnam. At least we weren't spit on. We were just ignored. But it gave you the feeling you were a sucker to have gone over there, that going to Korea wasn't important enough to give up the chance to get a good job at home."[169]

A Place of Remembrance

The Korean conflict remained virtually forgotten until the 1990s. Then, victory in Operation Desert Storm rekindled America's pride in her military. It also drew attention to the sacrifice of veterans of all wars, including those who fought in

Korea. Many Americans realized the latter had been treated unfairly, and felt that the time had come to honor them and to set aside a place of remembrance for them in the nation's capital. In 1992 construction began on the Korean War Veterans Memorial, located on the Mall in Washington, D.C.

In 1995 the monument was revealed as a multicomponent work. A short distance from the Lincoln Memorial, it features nineteen battle-ready soldiers, over seven feet tall and sculpted of roughened stainless steel, who appear to move in a V-formation through a carpet of juniper bushes (designed to resemble the rough terrain of Korea).

The figures are ethnically diverse and represent all branches of the military. Beside them runs a wall of polished granite into which has been sandblasted the images of those who provided support to the ground troops in the war. From a distance, these images blend together to form the shapes of Korea's hills and mountains. The motto "Freedom Is Not Free" is etched

The nineteen steel soldiers of the Korean War Veterans Memorial in Washington, D.C., honor the troops that fought in the conflict.

into a separate wall that stands near a pool of remembrance toward which the figures are facing. A granite curb with the names of the twenty-two nations that participated in the UN effort is also a part of the memorial.

With thousands of veterans in attendance, President Bill Clinton dedicated the memorial on July 27, 1995: "To all the veterans here today, and to all throughout our land who are watching, let us all say, when darkness threatened you kept the torch of liberty alight. You kept the flame burning so that others all across the world could share it. You showed the truth inscribed on the wall, that freedom is not free."[170]

More honor was given to Korean War veterans in the year 2000, the fiftieth anniversary of the outbreak of the conflict. During a commemoration period that ran from June 25, 2000, through November 11, 2003, wreaths of remembrance were laid at Arlington National Cemetery and the Korean War Veterans Memorial. Symposiums, dinners, and awards ceremonies took place. The Inchon invasion was reenacted in Norfolk, Virginia, and at Inchon, South Korea. Hundreds of ceremonies were held across the country. Groups such as the all-black Twenty-fourth Infantry Regiment and Puerto Rico's Sixty-fifth Infantry Regiment were recognized as well. "You made a powerful difference," army commander in chief Thomas A. Schwartz said to a group of veterans who revisited South Korea in the fall of 2000. "Historians call your war 'the forgotten war.' They

could not be more wrong. The vibrant achievements of the South Korean people ensure you will never be forgotten. Your courage and sacrifice secured the blessings of liberty for the South Korean people."[171]

A Greater Victory

Because of the memorial and other commemorative events, Americans who once overlooked the Korean War are now aware that it was a significant historical event. Nevertheless, to many it remains an unex-

Harry S. Truman (pictured) is remembered for abruptly relieving General MacArthur of his command during the Korean War.

plored chapter of American history. They still have little knowledge of the battles that were won and lost there. They do not know all the hardships that the fighting men endured. They have little notion of the scars the conflict left on men's bodies and souls. As Lieutenant Colonel Thomas Vance points out, "Many Americans remember only two salient [prominent] facts about the Korean War: We did not win it decisively, and a hero of World War Two, General Douglas MacArthur, was abruptly relieved of his command by President Truman."[172]

Those who are more familiar with the war hope that one day that will change. America owes respect and remembrance to the men who were the predecessors of those who still stand guard on the DMZ. As President Clinton said in an address in July 1995:

> Now we know, with the benefit of history, that those of you who served . . . laid the foundation for one of the greatest triumphs in the history of human freedom. By sending a clear message that America had not defeated fascism to see communism prevail, you put the Free World on the road to victory in the Cold War. That is your enduring contribution.[173]

Korean War veterans, most of whom are now more than seventy years old, remain characteristically modest about their contribution. They are from a generation that does not boast about its achievements and does not talk about its feelings. Nevertheless, they are gratified that the war is being remembered. "We are no longer forgotten. . . . Americans have finally realized that this was a war. Bullets were flying and people were dying and it was an actual war,"[174] says Major Carlo DePorto.

They are also proud of the legacy they leave behind. With their help, democracy emerged victorious when the Cold War ended in 1991. America continues to stand for peace and freedom. And those who served in the "forgotten war" are increasingly valued and respected for the sacrifices they made. "I am honored to have served here," says Joseph F. Shearer, who returned to Korea for the fiftieth anniversary in June 2000. "Whatever I did, however small it was, I thought it was worth the sacrifices."[175]

America has come to think so as well.

☆ Notes ☆

Introduction: The War That Never Was

1. Joseph C. Goulden, *Korea: The Untold Story of the War.* New York: Times, 1982, p. xxvi.
2. Harry S. Truman, 1951 State of the Union Address, "Historic Wartime Addresses," Northern Star Online. www.star.niu.edu.
3. Quoted in Donald Knox, *The Korean War: Pusan to Chosin.* San Diego: Harcourt Brace Jovanovich, 1985, p. 15.
4. Quoted in Aaron Brown and Michael James, "The Forgotten War," June 25, 2000, ABC News. http://abcnews.go.com.
5. Quoted in Goulden, *Korea,* p. xv.
6. Quoted in Goulden, *Korea,* p. 3.
7. Quoted in Richard K. Kolb, "War in a 'Land That Time Forgot': Korea 1950–1953," *VFW Magazine,* December 1991, Korean War Educator. www.koreanwar-educator.org.
8. Quoted in Kolb, "War in a 'Land That Time Forgot.'"

Chapter 1: Prologue to Action

9. Quoted in Robert Leckie, *The Wars of America.* New York: Harper & Row, 1968, p. 866.
10. Quoted in Richard K. Kolb, "Korea Before the War, 1945–1949," *VFW Magazine,* April 2000, Veterans of Foreign Wars. www.vfw.org.
11. Quoted in Knox, *The Korean War: Pusan to Chosin,* p. 6.
12. Harry S. Truman, *Memoirs by Harry S. Truman: Years of Trial and Hope.* Garden City, NY: Doubleday, 1956, pp. 332–33.
13. Harry S. Truman, "The President's News Conference of June 29, 1950," Truman Presidential Museum and Library. www.trumanlibrary.org.
14. Quoted in "Thoughts on Risk Taking," 2003, Jim McCormick website. www.takerisks.com.
15. Quoted in Knox, *The Korean War: Pusan to Chosin,* p. 214.
16. Harry S. Truman, "Speeches—Harry S. Truman," History Channel. www.historychannel.com.
17. Quoted in "General Matthew B. Ridgway (1895–1993)," PBS Online. www.pbs.org.
18. Quoted in Donald Knox, *The Korean War: Uncertain Victory.* San Diego: Harcourt Brace Jovanovich, 1988, p. 406.
19. Quoted in "Korean War Starts," Korea Web Weekly. www.kimsoft.com.
20. Quoted in Rudy Tomedi, *No Bugles, No Drums: An Oral History of the Korean War.* New York: John Wiley & Sons, 1993, p. 1.

21. Quoted in Steve Vogel, "The Forgotten War," *Washington Post*, June 19, 2000, University of Kansas Korean War Archive. www.ku.edu.
22. Anthony B. Herbert, *Herbert: The Making of a Soldier.* New York: Hippocrene, 1982, p. 13.
23. Quoted in Tomedi, *No Bugles, No Drums*, pp. 26–27.
24. Quoted in Tom McAnally, "Profile: Civil Rights Activist Rev. James Lawson," *Call*, March 21, 2003, Call Internet Edition. www.kccall.com.
25. Quoted in Tomedi, *No Bugles, No Drums*, p. 31.
26. Quoted in Goulden, *Korea*, p. xv.
27. Quoted in Knox, *The Korean War: Pusan to Chosin*, p. 96.

Chapter 2: A Shaky Beginning

28. Quoted in Marguerite Higgins, *War in Korea.* New York: Doubleday, 1951, p. 221.
29. Quoted in Vogel, "The Forgotten War."
30. Quoted in Tomedi, *No Bugles, No Drums*, p. 7.
31. "Memoir of Jake Huffaker," Korean War Educator. www.koreanwar-educator.org.
32. Quoted in Tomedi, *No Bugles, No Drums*, p. 4.
33. James Brady, *The Coldest War: A Memoir of Korea.* New York: Orion, 1990, p. 3.
34. Quoted in Knox, *The Korean War: Pusan to Chosin*, p. 238.

35. Quoted in Knox, *The Korean War: Pusan to Chosin*, p. 288.
36. Quoted in Knox, *The Korean War: Pusan to Chosin*, p. 293.
37. Quoted in Brandt Athey, "Korea and the 1950s," Yahoo!Geocities. www.geocities.com.
38. Quoted in Knox, *The Korean War: Pusan to Chosin*, p. 89.
39. Quoted in Tomedi, *No Bugles, No Drums*, p. 3.
40. Quoted in Knox, *The Korean War: Pusan to Chosin*, p. 454.
41. Quoted in Knox, *The Korean War: Pusan to Chosin*, p. 55.
42. Quoted in Knox, *The Korean War: Pusan to Chosin*, p. 58.
43. Quoted in Tomedi, *No Bugles, No Drums*, p. 20.
44. Quoted in Knox, *The Korean War: Pusan to Chosin*, p. 55.
45. Quoted in Knox, *The Korean War: Pusan to Chosin*, p. 383.
46. Quoted in Knox, *The Korean War: Pusan to Chosin*, p. 205.
47. Brady, "The Coldest War, p. 19.
48. Quoted in Knox, *The Korean War: Pusan to Chosin*, p. 206.
49. Quoted in Knox, *The Korean War: Pusan to Chosin*, p. 165.
50. Quoted in Knox, *The Korean War: Pusan to Chosin*, p. 391.

Chapter 3: To the Yalu and Back

51. Quoted in Knox, *The Korean War: Pusan to Chosin*, p. 208.
52. Quoted in Knox, *The Korean War:*

Pusan to Chosin, p. 419.

53. Quoted in Knox, *The Korean War: Pusan to Chosin*, p. 292.

54. Quoted in Knox, *The Korean War: Pusan to Chosin*, p. 411.

55. Quoted in Andrew Carroll, ed., *War Letters: Extraordinary Correspondence from American Wars*. New York: Scribner, 2001, p. 344.

56. Quoted in Knox, *The Korean War: Uncertain Victory*, p. 72.

57. Quoted in Knox, *The Korean War: Pusan to Chosin*, p. 541.

58. John A. Sullivan, *Toy Soldiers: Memoir of a Combat Platoon Leader in Korea*. Jefferson, NC: McFarland, 1991, p.70.

59. Quoted in Knox, *The Korean War: Pusan to Chosin*, p. 133.

60. David C. Hackworth, "Landmines: The Indiscriminate Killers," December 1996, Lawrence Coalition for Peace and Justice, University of Kansas. http://people.ku.edu.

61. Quoted in Knox, *The Korean War: Pusan to Chosin*, p. 107.

62. Quoted in Knox, *The Korean War: Pusan to Chosin*, p. 108.

63. Quoted in Knox, *The Korean War: Pusan to Chosin*, p. 317.

64. Quoted in Knox, *The Korean War: Pusan to Chosin*, p. 597.

65. Herbert, *Herbert: The Making of a Soldier*, pp. 56–57.

66. Quoted in Knox, *The Korean War: Pusan to Chosin*, p. 438.

67. Quoted in Knox, *The Korean War: Pusan to Chosin*, p. 124.

68. Quoted in Knox, *The Korean War: Pusan to Chosin*, p. 458.

69. Quoted in Knox, *The Korean War: Pusan to Chosin*, p. 585.

70. Quoted in Knox, *The Korean War: Pusan to Chosin*, p. 396.

71. Brady, *The Coldest War*, p. 117.

72. Quoted in Knox, *The Korean War: Pusan to Chosin*, p. 425.

73. Quoted in Tomedi, *No Bugles, No Drums*, p. 63.

74. Quoted in Knox, *The Korean War: Pusan to Chosin*, p. 600.

75. Quoted in Carroll, *War Letters*, pp. 335–36.

76. Higgins, *War in Korea*, p. 195.

77. Quoted in Knox, *The Korean War: Pusan to Chosin*, p. 558.

78. Quoted in Knox, *The Korean War: Pusan to Chosin*, p. 611.

79. Quoted in Knox, *The Korean War: Uncertain Victory*, p. 24.

80. Brady, *The Coldest War*, p. 2.

Chapter 4: Fighting the Bunker War

81. Quoted in Knox, *The Korean War: Uncertain Victory*, p. 211.

82. Quoted in Knox, *The Korean War: Uncertain Victory*, p. 310.

83. Quoted in Kolb, "War in a 'Land That Time Forgot.'"

84. Herb Renner, "The Korean Trenchwar: A Corpsman's Perspective," August 25, 2000, Korean War Photo-Documentary. www.rt66.com.

85. Quoted in Kolb, "War in a 'Land That Time Forgot.'"

86. Renner, "The Korean Trenchwar."

87. Martin Russ, *The Last Parallel: A Marine's War Journal*. New York: Fromm International, 1999, p. 240.

88. Quoted in Arthur W. Wilson, ed., *Korean Vignettes: Faces of War*. Portland, OR: Artwork, 1996, p. 377.

89. Quoted in Knox, *The Korean War: Uncertain Victory*, p. 310.

90. Quoted in Tomedi, *No Bugles, No Drums*, p. 144.

91. Quoted in Knox, *The Korean War: Uncertain Victory*, p. 312.

92. Quoted in Knox, *The Korean War: Uncertain Victory*, p. 314.

93. Quoted in Hal Barker, "Return to Heartbreak Ridge," Korean War Project. www.koreanwar.org.

94. Quoted in Knox, *The Korean War: Uncertain Victory*, p. 259.

95. Renner, "The Korean Trenchwar."

96. Quoted in Knox, *The Korean War: Uncertain Victory*, p. 263.

97. Bob Markey Sr., "My Life in the Seabees," March 6, 1998, MCB-10 Korea Seabees. http://mcb10korea seabees. net.

98. Quoted in Knox, *The Korean War: Uncertain Victory*, p. 261.

99. Quoted in Knox, *The Korean War: Uncertain Victory*, p. 264.

100. Quoted in Knox, *The Korean War: Uncertain Victory*, p. 408.

101. Quoted in Knox, *The Korean War: Pusan to Chosin*, p. 475.

102. Herbert, *Herbert*, p. 60.

103. Brady, *The Coldest War*, p. 132.

104. Brady, *The Coldest War*, p. 63.

105. Russ, *The Last Parallel*, p. 329.

106. Russ, *The Last Parallel*, p. 329.

107. "January 1953," Bob Dean's Korea: 1952–1953. www.mindspring.com.

108. Russ, *The Last Parallel*, p. 319.

109. Quoted in Knox, *The Korean War: Uncertain Victory*, p. 23.

Chapter 5: 24/7 Support

110. Quoted in Louis A. Arana-Barradas, "Just an Average Joe," *Airman*, April 2001, U.S. Air Force. www.af.mil.

111. Quoted in Knox, *The Korean War: Uncertain Victory*, p. 236.

112. Quoted in Knox, *The Korean War: Uncertain Victory*, pp. 237–38.

113. Quoted in Tomedi, *No Bugles, No Drums*, p. 165.

114. Quoted in Tomedi, *No Bugles, No Drums*, pp. 165–66.

115. Quoted in Barker, "Return to Heartbreak Ridge."

116. Quoted in Barker, "Return to Heartbreak Ridge."

117. Quoted in Knox, *The Korean War: Pusan to Chosin*, p. 45.

118. Quoted in Albert E. Cowdrey, "United States Army in the Korean War—the Medics' War," The MASH Movie Page. www.geocities.com.

119. Quoted in Rudi Williams, "Retired Army Nurse Recalls Korean War Service," March 30, 2001, U.S. Department of Defense. www.defenselink.mil.

120. Quoted in "Nurse Home from Korea Pleads for 'More Blood,'" Korean War

Veterans National Museum and Library. www.theforgottenvictory.org.

121. Markey, "My Life in the Seabees."

122. Markey, "My Life in the Seabees."

123. Quoted in Rod Paschall, *Witness to War: Korea.* New York: Berkley, 1995, p. 147.

124. Quoted in Tomedi, *No Bugles, No Drums,* p. 46.

125. Quoted in Tomedi, *No Bugles, No Drums,* p. 47.

126. Quoted in Knox, *The Korean War: Uncertain Victory,* p. 275.

127. Quoted in Knox, *The Korean War: Uncertain Victory,* p. 280.

128. Quoted in Wilson, *Korean Vignettes,* p. 343.

129. Quoted in Knox, *The Korean War: Uncertain Victory,* p. 62.

130. Herbert, *Herbert,* p. 19.

131. Quoted in Knox, *The Korean War: Uncertain Victory,* p. 372.

Chapter 6: Sick and Tired

132. Quoted in Knox, *The Korean War: Pusan to Chosin,* p. 369.

133. Quoted in Tomedi, *No Bugles, No Drums,* p. 59.

134. Quoted in Brady, *The Coldest War,* p. 135.

135. Quoted in Knox, *The Korean War: Pusan to Chosin,* p. 95.

136. Brady, *The Coldest War,* p. 118.

137. Quoted in Carroll, *War Letters,* p. 341.

138. Quoted in Tomedi, *No Bugles, No Drums,* p. 186.

139. Quoted in Knox, *The Korean War: Pusan to Chosin,* p. 529.

140. Quoted in Knox, *The Korean War: Uncertain Victory,* p. 67.

141. Quoted in Knox, *The Korean War: Pusan to Chosin,* p. 339.

142. Quoted in Knox, *The Korean War: Pusan to Chosin,* p. 94.

143. Quoted in Knox, *The Korean War: Pusan to Chosin,* p. 94.

144. Quoted in Knox, *The Korean War: Pusan to Chosin,* p. 462.

145. Quoted in Knox, *The Korean War: Uncertain Victory,* p. 361.

146. Quoted in Stanley Weintraub, *MacArthur's War: Korea and the Undoing of an American Hero.* New York: Free, 2000, p. 81.

147. Quoted in Tomedi, *No Bugles, No Drums,* p. 183.

148. Quoted in Nathan Stanley, "Transcript for the Interview with Grant Hauskins," Pacific University Asian Studies. http://mcel.pacificu.edu.

149. Quoted in Tomedi, *No Bugles, No Drums,* p. 202.

150. Quoted in Tomedi, *No Bugles, No Drums,* p. 201.

151. Quoted in Knox, *The Korean War: Pusan to Chosin,* p. 98.

152. Quoted in Tomedi, *No Bugles, No Drums,* p. 59.

153. Quoted in Knox, *The Korean War: Uncertain Victory,* p. 337.

154. Quoted in Indira A.R. Lakshmanan, "Rediscovering Pvt. Ryan," *Boston Globe,* June 25, 1999, Hill 303 Massacre. www.rt66.com.

155. Quoted in Knox, *The Korean War: Pusan to Chosin*, pp. 118–19.

156. Quoted in "Reliable Sources? Examining the Discrepancies in Eyewitness Accounts," May 12, 2000, US News. com. www.usnews.com.

157. Quoted in "No Gun Ri: Clinton's Statement," January 11, 2001, Online Newshour. www.pbs.org.

158. Quoted in Knox, *The Korean War: Uncertain Victory*, p. 354.

159. Quoted in Wilson, *Korean Vignettes*, p. 257.

Chapter 7: The Forgotten War

160. Quoted in Carroll, *War Letters*, p. 365.

161. Quoted in Robert J. Dvorchak, *Battle for Korea: The Associated Press History of the Conflict in Korea*. Conshohocken, PA: Combined, 1993, p. 281.

162. Quoted in Dvorchak, *Battle for Korea*, p. 282.

163. Quoted in "Korean War Memories —Class of 1951 Veterans Recall Life as Young Soldiers," *Clarkson University Magazine*, Winter 2002, Clarkson University. www.clarkson.edu.

164. Quoted in Knox, *The Korean War: Uncertain Victory*, p. 354.

165. Quoted in Dvorchak, *Battle for Korea*, p. 289.

166. Quoted in Jeff Decker, "Korean War Anniversary," June 25, 2000, U.S. Legacies. www.uslegacies.org.

167. Quoted in Knox, *The Korean War: Uncertain Victory*, p. 372.

168. Quoted in Wilson, *Korean Vignettes*, p. 275.

169. Quoted in Tomedi, *No Bugles, No Drums*, p. 156.

170. "Remarks by President Clinton and President Kim of South Korea at Dedication of Korean War Veterans Memorial," July 27, 1995, Korean War Project. www.koreanwar.org.

171. Quoted in Frances Trexler, "Widow of Soldier Travels to Korea for Ceremonies Marking War's 50th Anniversary," *Salisbury Post*, November 17, 2000. www.salisburypost.com.

172. Thomas J. Vance, "Remembering the Heroes of America's Forgotten War," April 1998, Army Public Affairs Website. www.dtic.mil.

173. Quoted in Vance, "Remembering the Heroes of America's Forgotten War."

174. Quoted in "Soundoff!" U.S. Army Garrison Fort Meade. www. ftmeade. army.mil.

175. Quoted in Sang-Hun Choe, "Veterans Return to Korea," *Laredo Morning Times*, June 4, 2000. www.lmtonline.com.

★ Glossary ★

AWOL: Absent without leave; the military term for a less serious form of desertion.

battle fatigue: Stress disorder resulting from combat.

breakout: To fight one's way to safety.

bugout: To retreat in confusion.

bunker: An earthen fortification, mostly or entirely below ground.

Cold War: Political struggle between the United States and the Soviet Union, coupled with a buildup of military weaponry, spying, propaganda, and political deception.

Democratic People's Republic of Korea (DPRK): North Korea.

Demilitarized Zone (DMZ): A stretch of land dividing the Democratic People's Republic of Korea (North Korea) and the Republic of Korea (South Korea).

domino theory: The presumption that if one country's government falls to communism, the governments of neighboring nations will soon topple like a row of dominoes.

guerrilla: A member of an irregular armed force that fights a stronger force by sabotage and harassment. Also, unconventional tactics such as sabotage and harassment.

infantry: The branch of an army made up of units trained to fight on foot.

limited warfare: Warfare that does not utilize all possible tactics and force.

MiG: Soviet-made fighter jets flown by the North Koreans during the war.

MiG Alley: Airspace directly south of the Yalu River in North Korea.

Mobile Army Surgical Hospital (MASH): Mobile hospitals set up behind the lines to provide early treatment of illness and injury.

point: Position held by the first man in line on a patrol.

post-traumatic stress disorder: A psychological condition characterized by flashbacks, nightmares, anxiety, social withdrawal, and other symptoms, affecting individuals who have experienced or witnessed profoundly traumatic events.

reconnaissance: Exploration or scouting.

Republic of Korea (ROK): South Korea.

reserve: A period of time behind the lines to rest and unwind.

rotation: Point system by which soldiers qualified to leave Korea.

Tenth (X) Corps: Army and marine units led by General Edmund Almond in the Inchon invasion.

38th parallel: A line of latitude that runs around the earth parallel to and 38 degrees north of the equator. One degree of latitude measures about sixty nine miles on the earth's surface.

trenchfoot: A fungal infection in which the foot becomes red, swollen, and sore.

United Service Organization (USO): Organization that provides morale, welfare, and recreational services to uniformed military personnel.

★ For Further Reading ★

Brent Ashabranner, *Remembering Korea: The Korean War Veterans Memorial.* Brookfield, CT: Twenty-First Century, 2001. A well-written account of the development of the Korean War Veterans Memorial.

Maurice Isserman, *The Korean War: America at War.* New York: Facts On File, 1992. Acquaints the reader with the events of the Korean War.

Conrad R. Stein, *The Korean War: "The Forgotten War."* Berkeley Heights, NJ: Enslow, 1994. Another clear and concise overview of the Korean War.

Michael V. Uschan, *The Korean War.* San Diego: Lucent, 2001. Korean War overview with additional emphasis on the political climate at home during the early 1950s. Includes a timeline.

★ Works Consulted ★

Books

Lee Ballenger, *The Outpost War: U.S. Marines in Korea, Vol. 1: 1952*. Washington, DC: Brassey's, 2000. The book focuses on the Marine Corps' combat operations during the later years of the Korean War.

James Brady, *The Coldest War: A Memoir of Korea*. New York: Orion, 1990. A soldier's thoughtful perspective during the bunker phase of the war. Excellent.

Andrew Carroll, ed., *War Letters: Extraordinary Correspondence from American Wars*. New York: Scribner, 2001. A collection of previously unpublished letters from men in war. One chapter is dedicated to the Korean War.

Robert J. Dvorchak, *Battle for Korea: The Associated Press History of the Conflict in Korea*. Conshohocken, PA: Combined, 1993. A historical account of the war written by Associated Press war correspondents. Illustrated with pictures by AP photographers who followed the battles.

Joseph C. Goulden, *Korea: The Untold Story of the War*. New York: Times, 1982. This account of the war uses the personal notes of Matthew Ridgway, the memoirs of Douglas MacArthur's aide, secret war files of the National Security Council, and other valuable source material.

Anthony B. Herbert, *Herbert: The Making of a Soldier*. New York: Hippocrene, 1982. Herbert, an enthusiastic participant in the war, provides a unique perspective on life as a soldier.

Marguerite Higgins, *War in Korea*. New York: Doubleday, 1951. A female war correspondent's reports from the front lines of the Korean War.

Donald Knox, *The Korean War: Pusan to Chosin*. San Diego: Harcourt Brace Jovanovich, 1985. Hundreds of veterans from Korea give accounts of their term of service during the first months of the Korean War. Easy and exciting to read.

———, *The Korean War: Uncertain Victory*. San Diego: Harcourt Brace Jovanovich, 1988. Veterans of the Korean War give accounts of their term of service during the last years of the conflict in this companion to Knox's oral history of the early war. Both works provide excellent insight into the war from soldiers' perspectives.

Robert Leckie, *The Wars of America*. New York: Harper & Row, 1968. A comprehensive overview of war in the United

States up to the Vietnam era. The Korean War chapter gives background on the war as well as an interesting overview of the conflict.

Rod Paschall, *Witness to War: Korea.* New York: Berkley, 1995. A collection of primary source documents and narratives from the Korean War.

Martin Russ, *The Last Parallel: A Marine's War Journal.* New York: Fromm International, 1999. Russ tells the story of his service in Korea from 1952 to 1953.

John A. Sullivan, *Toy Soldiers: Memoir of a Combat Platoon Leader in Korea.* Jefferson, NC: McFarland, 1991. Another fascinating account of the war from a soldier's perspective.

Rudy Tomedi, *No Bugles, No Drums: An Oral History of the Korean War.* New York: John Wiley & Sons, 1993. Descriptions of various aspects of the war through the eyes of those who fought there. An excellent first-person source.

Harry S. Truman, *Memoirs by Harry S. Truman: Years of Trial and Hope.* Garden City, NY: Doubleday, 1956. In the second of two volumes, Truman discusses the Korean War in depth, including his feelings about the conflict, background discussions with his advisers, and difficulties with General MacArthur.

Stanley Weintraub, *MacArthur's War: Korea and the Undoing of an American Hero.* New York: Free, 2000. An account of Douglas MacArthur's leadership in the Korean War.

Arthur W. Wilson, ed., *Korean Vignettes: Faces of War.* Portland, OR: Artwork, 1996. More than two hundred veterans of the Korean War recall their experiences and thoughts on topics ranging from can openers to combat.

Internet Sources

Louis A. Arana-Barradas, "Just an Average Joe," *Airman*, April 2001, U.S. Air Force. www.af.mil.

Brandt Athey, "Korea and the 1950s," Yahoo!Geocities. www.geocities.com.

Hal Barker, "Return to Heartbreak Ridge," Korean War Project. www.koreanwar.org.

Aaron Brown and Michael James, "The Forgotten War," June 25, 2000, ABC News. http://abcnews.go.com.

Sang-Hun Choe, "Veterans Return to Korea," *Laredo Morning Times*, June 4, 2000. www.lmtonline.com.

Albert E. Cowdrey, "United States Army in the Korean War—the Medics' War," The MASH Movie Page. www.geocities. com.

Jeff Decker, "Korean War Anniversary," June 25, 2000, U.S. Legacies. www.uslegacies.org.

General Matthew B. Ridgway (1895–1993), PBS Online. www.pbs.org.

David C. Hackworth, "Landmines: The Indiscriminate Killers," December 1996, Lawrence Coalition for Peace and Justice, University of Kansas. http://people.ku.edu.

"Interview with Lt. Col. Charles Bussey—3/2/97," CNN's Cold War Series. www.cnn.com.

"January 1953," Bob Dean's Korea: 1952–1953. www.mindspring.com.

Richard K. Kolb, "Korea Before the War, 1945–1949," *VFW Magazine*, April 2000, Veterans of Foreign Wars. www.vfw.org.

————, "War in a 'Land That Time Forgot': Korea 1950–1953," *VFW Magazine*, December 1991, Korean War Educator. www.koreanwar-educator.org.

"Korean War Memories—Class of 1951 Veterans Recall Life as Young Soldiers," *Clarkson University Magazine*, Winter 2002, Clarkson University. www.clarkson.edu.

"Korean War Starts," Korea Web Weekly. www.kimsoft.com.

"Korean War Vets Must Not Be Forgotten," *East Brunswick Sentinel*, July 12, 2000. http://ebs.gmnews.com.

Indira A.R. Lakshmanan, "Rediscovering Pvt. Ryan," *Boston Globe*, June 25, 1999, Hill 303 Massacre. www.rt66.com.

Douglas MacArthur, "Farewell Address to Congress," April 19, 1951, *American Rhetoric*. www.americanrhetoric.com.

Bob Markey Sr., "My Life in the Seabees," March 6, 1998, MCB-10 Korea Seabees. http://mcb10koreaseabees.net.

Tom McAnally, "Profile: Civil Rights Activist Rev. James Lawson," *Call*, March 21, 2003, Call Internet Edition. www.kccall.com.

"Memoir of Jake Huffaker," Korean War Educator. www.koreanwar-educator.org.

"No Gun Ri: Clinton's Statement," January 11, 2001, Online Newshour. www.pbs.org.

"Nurse Home from Korea Pleads for 'More Blood,'" Korean War Veterans National Museum and Library. www.theforgottenvictory.org.

"Reliable Sources? Examining the Discrepancies in Eyewitness Accounts," May 12, 2000, USNews.com. www.usnews.com.

"Remarks by President Clinton and President Kim of South Korea at Dedication of Korean War Veterans Memorial," July 27, 1995, Korean War Project. www.koreanwar.org.

Herb Renner, "The Korean Trenchwar: A Corpsman's Perspective," August 25, 2000, Korean War Photo-Documentary. www.rt66.com.

"Soundoff!" U.S. Army Garrison Fort Meade. www.ftmeade.army.mil.

Nathan Stanley, "Transcript for the Interview with Grant Hauskins," Pacific University Asian Studies. http://mcel.pacificu.edu.

"Thoughts on Risk Taking," 2003, Jim McCormick website. www.takerisks.com.

Frances Trexler, "Widow of Soldier Travels to Korea for Ceremonies Marking War's 50th Anniversary," *Salisbury Post*, November 17, 2000. www.salisburypost.com.

Harry S. Truman, 1951 State of the Union Address, "Historic Wartime Addresses,"

Northern Star Online. www.star.niu. edu.

———,"Speeches—Harry S. Truman," History Channel. www.historychannel.com

———,"The President's News Conference of June 29, 1950," Truman Presidential Museum and Library. www.trumanlibrary.org.

Thomas J. Vance, "Remembering the Heroes of America's Forgotten War,"

April 1998, Army Public Affairs Website. www.dtic.mil.

Steve Vogel, "The Forgotten War," *Washington Post,* June 19, 2000, University of Kansas Korean War Archive. www.ku.edu.

Rudi Williams, "Retired Army Nurse Recalls Korean War Service," March 30, 2001, U.S. Department of Defense. www.defenselink.mil.

☆ Index ☆

★ Picture Credits ★

Cover: © Bettmann/CORBIS
AP/Wide World Photos, 46, 53
© Bettmann/CORBIS, 35, 38, 41, 79, 84
© CORBIS, 26, 33, 49, 68, 73, 80
© Hulton/Archive by Getty Images, 13 (left and right), 18, 24,
    58, 62
© Hulton Deutsch Collection/CORBIS, 47
© Wally McNamee/CORBIS, 89
National Archives, 16, 29, 64, 77, 85
Brandy Noon, 8, 12
© Time Life Pictures by Getty Images, 52, 61, 67, 88
U.S. Army, 30
U.S. Army/Courtesy Harry S. Truman Library, 90
Steve Zmina, 15
© Jim Zuckerman/CORBIS, 42

★ About the Author ★

Diane Yancey works as a freelance writer in the Pacific Northwest, where she has lived for over twenty years. She writes nonfiction for middle-grade and high school readers, and enjoys traveling and collecting old books. Some of her other books for Lucent include *Strategic Battles* (Civil War Library), *Life of an American Soldier* (Vietnam War Library), and *Leaders and Generals* and *Life of an American Soldier in Afghanistan* (War on Terrorism Library).